SOME
PROFESSIONAL RECOLLECTIONS.

BY A FORMER MEMBER OF

THE COUNCIL OF THE INCORPORATED
LAW SOCIETY.

LONDON:

RICHARD BENTLEY AND SON,

Publishers in Ordinary to Her Majesty the Queen.

1883.

270. c. 49.

INTRODUCTION.

It has been asserted, with truth, that every successful man, in whatever station, who has raised himself to independence by honourable self-exertion, ought to feel proud of the result; and that any faithful statement of the course he has followed, and of the events which may have occurred or in which he has taken part whilst engaged in the battle of life, cannot fail to be interesting to the general reader. "Just as every pawn is necessary in a game of chess," observes a recent writer by way of apology for her memoirs, "so the humblest individual fills a part in the great stage of life which no other person, however superior in talent or capacity, could fill."

To this wide-spread feeling we no doubt owe

the numerous autobiographies which of late
years have issued from the press—sometimes
boldly published by the author himself in his
lifetime, sometimes kept back in his desk and
not given to the world till after his death.
The advantage in the former case is that the
final revision is his own. The style and
arrangement are often the best illustration
of the influence of the very experiences he
describes. Not so where, after the author's
death, the crude manuscript, seldom revised
for publication, is placed in the hands of an
editor. Such an autobiography, especially if
kept in the form of a diary, often conveys the
impressions of mere momentary impulse or
prejudice, so that the editor has the delicate
and responsible task cast on him, either of
suppressing passages at the risk of destroying
the natural character of the author, or of
giving offence by the too indiscriminate use
of his materials.

Of autobiographies published by living men
we have lately had one by a learned serjeant,

giving us the experiences, professional and otherwise, of his active life. If he has not told us the whole truth, he yet has given to the world an amusing book, the phraseology of which, from its ease, *insouciance*, and humour, is a reflex of the character of the man, whilst throughout its pages may be traced his sincere desire to do justice to his friends and to set down naught in malice.

It was the perusal of these volumes which first suggested to me the idea of describing in popular form a few cases which have come directly and personally within my own professional experience. The solicitor has more intercourse with actual life, and is brought more immediately into contact with human nature under its various forms than the barrister, who is supposed to know only what is put before him in his brief. Though members of the same honourable profession, their sphere of action, duties, and qualifications are separate and distinct. Long may they so continue for the good of the public.

At the same time the solicitor is more fettered by the obligation of secrecy, and a stricter duty is imposed upon him, in publishing, to use the matter he has at command with judgment.

I had not the courage to follow the example of the learned serjeant, and to attempt a connected autobiography. Nor would it have been worth reading if I had. After all, with most of us, it is but the fragments of our lives that will bear committing to record. I have therefore selected such cases only as I thought would interest the general reader, and could be made known without violating confidences. And to remove the possibility of objection on the latter score, I have, in some of the cases, substituted feigned names for the real ones. In all other respects, both as to facts and figures and all other details, I have endeavoured to adhere strictly to the truth.

Withdrawn as I now am from the busy world, it has been an amusement to me during my leisure hours to recall some of the scenes in which I took part, and in connection with which I made many of my most valued friends. "In old age alone," says the late Sir Archibald Alison in his autobiography, "we are masters of a treasure of which we cannot be deprived, the only treasure we can call our own. The pleasures of memory, and the retrospect of the varied images which in an active life have floated before the mind, compensate, and more than compensate, for the alternate pleasures and cares of active life."

CONTENTS.

A ROMANCE OF THE PEERAGE.

SOME

PROFESSIONAL RECOLLECTIONS.

A ROMANCE OF THE PEERAGE.

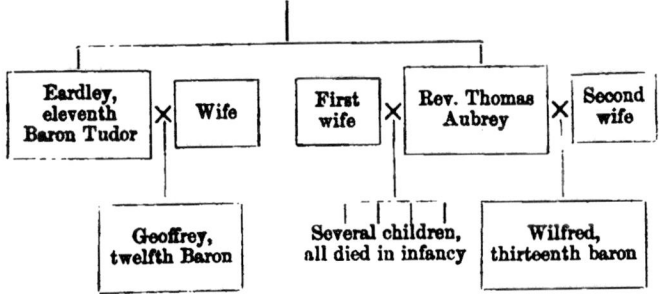

IF the reader were to turn over the pages of his Shakespeare he would be rewarded by finding embalmed, in one of the plays, an ancestor of the peer who is here called Wilfred Aubrey, thirteenth Baron Tudor. The title is one of the most ancient and honourable in the long roll of our nobles.

It holds a place in Magna Charta, in the troublous times of Henry VI., in the history of the Commonwealth, and has been transmitted without taint in unbroken descent to the present period, with every prospect, happily, of being perpetuated in favour of generations to follow.

It is sufficient for the present purpose, however, if, passing over the historical traditions connected with the family, the narrative commence with the two sons of the tenth Baron, namely, Eardley and Thomas.

Eardley succeeded to the title and became eleventh Baron Tudor. He lived to a very advanced age, and died in 1844, leaving one only son, Geoffrey, surviving him. Geoffrey Aubrey, twelfth Baron Tudor, died unmarried not many years ago. He himself inherited the title when in middle life, and enjoyed it after his father's death for some years, disappointing his friends by never marrying. Consequently, on his death without issue, the lineal descent failed, and the title had to be

traced back, through a period of upwards of
fifty years, to the collateral branch, namely,
to Thomas Aubrey, the younger brother of
Eardley.

We have, therefore, to follow the fortunes
of this younger brother, the Honourable
Thomas Aubrey. Like most younger sons of
old families under our system of primogeniture,
he had to seek a profession for his livelihood.
He graduated as a Bachelor of Arts at Oxford,
and took holy orders, beginning life by accepting a curacy in the west of England.
Marriage appears to be almost the inevitable
consequence of a curacy. He followed his
fate in that respect, and immediately married
a lady in his own rank of life, but without
fortune, taking her with him to his curacy,
and trusting to Providence to provide a suffi-
ciency for their joint support, and that of the
eventual family.

His wife bore him, as might be anticipated, several children, all of whom, fortunately perhaps for the parents in their

straitened circumstances, died successively in infancy.

By the early death of her children, Mrs. Aubrey was spared the cares and duties of maternity. The liberty thus accidentally given to her afforded her the opportunity for indulging her inborn passion for the stage. She had always had an ardent longing for that vocation, but her husband's profession, combined with the claims of a young family, had for some years restrained her.

Relieved by the death of all her children from the latter obligation, the passion became insuperable. Her husband remonstrated, as was natural. The stage in those days, especially in the eyes of the clergy belonging to a certain school of theology, whose prejudices have not altogether died out even now, was regarded as the resort only of the profane, and he was shocked at his wife indulging in such a depraved taste. He reasoned in vain. Finding remonstrance of no avail, and that she was bent on following her own inclinations, he insisted on a separation, the terms of which were formulated by deed.

Being thus free by mutual consent, she left her husband in his humble curacy in the west of England, and made her way to Dublin, where she was offered an engagement by Daly, then the manager of the Theatre Royal in that city.

Long afterwards, and only from the biography of a celebrated cotemporaneous actor, published at a comparatively recent date, it appeared that she played *Juliet* in that theatre to Holman's *Romeo*, and *Almeyda* to his *Dorax* in "Don Sebastian," and that the two also played together in "Fontainville Forest," "Venice Preserved," "Alexander," and other plays. We have modern examples of actors and actresses whose popularity was due to other attractions than their artistic merits ; and that the same was also true in Shakespeare's time we gather from what is said of the players in "Hamlet," "the trage-dians of the city," who, though "their en-

deavours kept wonted pace," were ousted from
public favour by a troop—"an aiery"—of
children, "little Eyases," who carried away
all the applause. So it may be presumed, as
nothing has been transmitted to us of Mrs.
Thomas Aubrey's dramatic fame, that her
chief attraction consisted in her name being
announced in the playbills with the prefix of
"honourable."

From Dublin she proceeded to **Edinburgh,**
where, fortunately, as will afterwards be seen,
a more accurate record of her performances
was preserved. She acted at the Theatre
Royal, Edinburgh, in the principal female
characters of many of Shakespeare's plays,
commencing with *Katherine* in "Taming the
Shrew," and afterwards travelled to York, to
fulfil theatrical engagements there, still always
being announced in the playbills by her own
name.

Now, whilst thus separated from her husband, and moving in an atmosphere more
dangerous to female virtue then than perhaps

it is in these reformed times, she made the acquaintance, when acting in Edinburgh, of a wealthy young merchant of that city, McFarlane by name, and consented to live with him as his wife.

The Honourable Thomas Aubrey was in due time made aware of the circumstances. But divorce in those days could only be obtained by Act of Parliament, and an Act of Parliament cost a sum of money to which his means were inadequate. Some will here be reminded of the sarcastic words of the late Mr. Justice Maule, in passing sentence on a poor labouring man, whose wife had run away from him, and who had married again and been convicted of bigamy— "Prisoner, you should first have brought an action and have recovered damages, and then have applied for an Act of Parliament to release you from your first wife. It might have cost you a thousand pounds; but the law makes no distinction between rich and poor!"—words which no doubt had their effect

in inducing the legislature (whether wisely or
not is another question) to pass a general Act
to bring divorce within reach of all classes.

The Honourable Thomas Aubrey was much
in the same position, except that, though poor
himself, he had a brother a peer, by whose
assistance he eventually was able to present
his petition to the Lords, and to prove his
case, and thus obtain a divorce by a special
Act of Parliament.

That Act having at length passed, he
married a second time, and was not sorry to
change the scene of his former domestic life
by accepting an archdeaconry in one of the
colonies, where he went with his second wife,
and where he resided many years, and ultimately died. By his second wife he had
several children, sons as well as daughters,
all of whom survived him, Wilfred Aubrey
being the eldest son of the second marriage,
and, at the time of the death of his cousin
Geoffrey, twelfth baron, a man of about fifty
years of age.

These events in the life of the Honourable Thomas Aubrey,—namely, his marriage and separation from his first wife, her misconduct, the divorce, and his second marriage,—all took place during the last century, and were forgotten, or regarded as things of the past, until upon the recent and rather unexpected death of Geoffrey, twelfth baron, it became necessary for his cousin, Wilfred Aubrey, to dive into the family history for the last sixty years or so, in order to establish his title to the peerage as the eldest son of the Honourable Thomas Aubrey.

The facts were collected with some difficulty, and, according to the requirements of the House of Lords, were submitted to the Lord Chancellor in proper documentary form, preparatory to the issuing of the writ which was to summon Wilfred Aubrey to the House of Lords as thirteenth Baron Tudor.

After a period of suspense, what was the Lord Chancellor's astounding announcement on these documents when they had been duly

.. could not be! Proof ha·
of the births and deaths of _al_·
the first marriage, of the divorc·
marriage, of the death of the ε·
of the birth of Wilfred, the elc·
second marriage; the proofs ·
" Not so," was the Lord Chε·
through his private secretary.
petition for the divorce, now
archives of the House, and you
it stated that the Honourable
Aubrey gave birth to a son, alleg·
to be the son of McFarlane, bu·
lock. The petition, you will fil·
the son may be declared to b·
The Divorce Act intentionallv·

sumed to be the son of the Honourable Thomas Aubrey. Where is that son? His death has not been proved."

Here was a startling discovery, bursting like a shell amongst the second family, none of whom, though aware, of course, of the divorce, had ever seen or heard of the petition on which it was founded and from whom all the discreditable facts connected with it had been studiously concealed.

The Lord Chancellor had, however, hit the blot; there was no escape from it. The son, born in the last century, the *de facto* issue of the adultery, but *de jure* issue of the first marriage, who had never been heard of before, whose very existence was unknown to any living member of the family, must be traced, and his death without leaving male issue proved; or if, perchance, still living, evidence must be dug out and produced to rebut the presumption of law that a son born whilst the husband is "within the four seas" is his lawful son.

be conclusively proved that by
could this son be the son of th
Thomas Aubrey.

Towards proof of non-access
Honourable Thomas Aubrey and
after she quitted the west of Eng
the first point of departure would
the deed of separation. But wh
deed? It had probably remai
possession of the husband, and
destroyed by him on his second
had been carried with him to
when he became archdeacon, and
At all events, it could not anywhe
but on untying some old bundle
covered with dust and cobwebs

a copy of the deed written on draft paper, yellow with age, and endorsed with the word "examined." This word was in the handwriting of one of the predecessors of the firm, who fortunately was still living, though of great age, and long retired from practice. He verified the copy, and that the endorsed word "examined" was his handwriting.

But if there was unexpected good fortune at the outset in meeting with an aged witness, who could still prove this important fact on which the case was to be based, what shall be said of the next happy coincidence?

McFarlane, the Edinburgh *Lothario* of the last century, was also ascertained to be alive, though very much beyond eighty years of age. He was residing with one of his married daughters in Yorkshire. How to approach him was a question for careful consideration. It was thought best to broach the subject to him at a personal interview, and without any previous preparation. The writer of these pages accordingly went down from London to

Tadcaster by rail overnight, and the next morning hired a carriage from the hotel to take him thence to the well-known old family seat, where the octogenarian gentleman was residing. On arriving at the house, the writer was ushered into the drawing-room, where fortunately no one but himself was present. Into this room, after a short time, Mr. McFarlane entered, with tottering steps, completely in the dark as to who his visitor was and the object of the visit. The preliminaries of the interview were ceremonious and embarrassing, but the old gentleman gradually thawed, and was at length prevailed upon, though with much reluctance, to converse on that epoch of his early youth. His narrative was as follows :—

That he became acquainted with the Honourable Mrs. Thomas Aubrey whilst she was acting in Edinburgh. He dated his first acquaintance with her when she took her benefit at the Theatre Royal. That night he remembered she played *Lady Macbeth*,

but he could not fix the precise day, no, nor
the precise month or year—his memory was a
perfect blank as to dates; that he certainly
did live with her afterwards both in Edinburgh
and York; that a son was born, whom he
maintained till the boy was thirteen or fourteen years of age, when, becoming involved in
his circumstances, he sent the boy to sea to
get rid of him; that some ten years or so
afterwards, on one winter's night, whilst
seated before the fire in his parlour in Edinburgh, a man, thickly dressed in the rough
garb of a common sailor, suddenly presented
himself before him, and asked to be recognized, but that he (McFarlane) refused to
have anything to say to him; that he gave
the man a trifle to carry him back to London,
since which he (McFarlane) said he had never
seen or heard anything of him.

Here, of course, was some valuable information; but how were the dates to be fixed?
To fix precisely, not only the years and
months, but the days, and to prove that

seemed cruel, even if it had be
insist upon taxing the memory (
considerably past eighty years
the precise dates of events wl
pened sixty years previously, ¡
hoped had been altogether buried
" Remember not the sins of my ;
always the refrain of his narrativ(

Whilst all means of arriving a
dates appeared to be beyond reacl
transpired that in the Advocate
Edinburgh all the playbills of
Royal had been preserved for a
These playbills had been bound
logically, and were extant in
They were searched, and furn

her own name during two or more consecutive
months. They showed also the characters
she filled each night and the actual night of
her benefit, confirming the impression vaguely
remembered by McFarlane, that on that particular night she played *Lady Macbeth*. Here,
then, was accurate proof that McFarlane and
Mrs. Thomas Aubrey were passing as man
and wife in Edinburgh at a given date fixed
by the playbills, and afterwards, by his own
admission, journeying together thence direct
to York, in order that she might fulfil her
theatrical engagements in the latter city.

But where was the husband during this
precise period of time ? There were no rail-
ways then, it is true, and to traverse three or
four hundred miles of road required more time
then than it does now ; but if he happened to
be anywhere " within the four seas " (as the
quaint indefinite phraseology of the law then
expressed it), the legal presumption of access
would be supported.

As a matter of fact, he had remained at his

become of great value hereaf
letters were discovered written
late Sir Alexander Johnstone, a1
friend, whose son had casually p1
These letters bore distinctly th
the village in the west of Eng
the letters were written, with th
they were posted, correspondir
earlier dates of the Edinburgh]

Then it appeared that from
England the Honourable Tho
had journeyed to Oxford to take
degree, which had been delaye
of means, and had thenceforwar
St. Mary Hall for two months.
secutively. But how could th

and unearthed the old battelling-books of that
date, containing entries of tea, coffee, rolls
and butter, chops, steaks, and other eatables
(technically called "battells") supplied to
him from day to day from the buttery of the
Hall, with the exact date and charge against
each item. The accident of the existence
of these books was the more remarkable,
as it is the well-known practice of most
of the colleges of Oxford to destroy such
records every two or three years as useless
lumber. The old manciple of the Hall,
Court, by name, happened also to be living,
perhaps one of the very few survivors of a
generation of men who have gained for Oxford
a reputation for longevity, and the last of
whom (Dr. Hawkins) may be said to have
only just passed away. He was able to
identify the Honourable Thomas Aubrey as
a resident at the Hall at the time specified,
and to refresh his memory as to dates by
reference to the old battelling-books. Following on the residence at St. Mary Hall

It is not pretended that th
solitary instance of important fa
having been elucidated and p
lapse of many years, by docume;
at the time as mere rubbish, fi
waste-paper basket or for the
light the fire with. Many simi
probably be called to mind, but
the less interesting on that acc
who have read Mark Napier's l
the great Marquis of Montrose
remember that much of the h
early life of the marquis is d
biographer from the simple ei
accounts of Master John Lamby
" Little," writes Mr. Napier, " d

even his faithful chaplain had omitted, and
which was destined not to be discovered until
two centuries after the hero's death." . As
little did the cook of St. Mary Hall suppose,
when making his entries in the battelling-
books of the Hall, that those simple records
of the kitchen were long afterwards to be
solemnly given in evidence in the House of
Lords and to furnish proof of the right of a
peer of ancient lineage to take his seat in that
august assembly. Opportunely, it may be
added, in every respect, were these simple
records discovered and produced, for St. Mary
Hall itself, dating from 1436, has now ceased
to enjoy a separate existence.

Such was the evidence which tended to
show the absolute separation of husband and
wife, both by deed and in fact, during the
critical period necessary for Wilfred's case.
The search for this evidence was warranted
and encouraged by some previous judicial
decisions, admitting proof to modify the old
rule of law which legitimized issue of the wife

so long as the husband was within "the four seas."

Of these decisions, perhaps, the case of the Barony of Gardner is as interesting as any. The Honourable Alan Gardner, afterwards second Lord Gardner, a captain in the navy, married, in March, 1796, Maria Adderley, and they cohabited together as man and wife until January, 1802. On the 30th of January, 1802, Captain Gardner took leave of his wife on board a frigate, which sailed from Portsmouth a few days afterwards for the West Indies. She accompanied him to Portsmouth to see the last of him, and there left him and returned to London. The ship made out her voyage to the West Indies, and returned to Portsmouth on the 11th of July in the same year, and Mrs. Gardner went to Portsmouth to greet her husband on his return. On the 8th of December in the same year, Mrs. Gardner gave birth to a son, who was christened Henry Fenton Gardner. Captain Gardner then obtained a divorce on evidence

which impeached his wife's conduct during his
absence at sea. In 1808 he succeeded to the
Barony of Gardner. In the following year he
married the Honourable Charlotte Smith, for
his second wife, and by her had a son, Alan
Legge Gardner, who was born in 1810. Lord
Gardner died in 1815, leaving Alan Legge
Gardner heir to the Barony, in the event
of Henry Fenton Gardner being illegitimate.
That question was carried to the House of
Lords, who, after hearing medical and other
evidence, resolved that Alan Legge Gardner
had made good his claim to the Barony as
the only son of his father, the former peer,
and that Henry Fenton Gardner, though born
before the divorce, was illegitimate.

But we have lost sight all this time of the
sailor. As to him there was no clue whatever,
except that he had been sent to sea whilst a
boy at the age of thirteen or fourteen, and had
not been heard of since, unless the man in
rough seaman's dress, who had suddenly appeared to McFarlane, whilst seated in his

avoided the subject as calculat
entail obligations on him whicl
now care to acknowledge, and
was unprepared.

It may be asked why inquire
the sailor, because, if by precis
proof of the husband being i
place and the wife in another, a
the two at a particular period v
then the existence of a son sub:
of the wife at a date which v
evidence, would be immaterial
question. It was, however, nec
in view that these proofs were
had to be submitted to the ordes
of Lords, and jealously scrutir

mittee to be insufficient, the case of Wilfred
Aubrey would fail, nor would he be in a position to resuscitate it until he could show that
the sailor was dead without leaving male issue.
If, on the other hand, the sailor were alive, it
was important he should be found and identified, so that at some future time when he did
die, and die without leaving male issue, the
claim of Wilfred might, on proof of those facts,
be revived.

Where, then, was the sailor ?   Was he alive
or dead ? and how could he, *filius nullius* as he
was, be traced ?   There is a register of seamen
kept at the Custom House in London, and to
search that register offered the obvious, and
indeed the only, hope of some clue being found
to him.   But, if living, what name would he
be likely to bear?   McFarlane was too canny
a Scot to allow the boy to bear his own
name, and there was, in fact, no entry in the
register under that name.   Under the name
of Charles Aubrey, however, a seaman had
been entered, and was apparently still in

the Mercantile Marine. Following up that
clue, it was ascertained that one Charles
Aubrey had not long before gone out in
the brig *Mary Anne*, Thomas Jones, master,
to the West Indies, as a seaman before the
mast. The ship at the time of inquiry was
supposed to have left the West Indies on her
return voyage, and her owners were requested
to report her arrival in the docks. The ship
duly arrived, her crew were immediately
mustered, and sure enough there was the man,
the very man himself. He was sent for and
promptly interrogated as to his birth, parent-
age, and education. He replied that he knew
little about himself under either head; that his
object throughout his life had been to find out
who he was; that he remembered being placed
at a school in Essex by a gentleman named
McFarlane, who was said to be his guardian, and
from that school he was suddenly taken away,
without any apparent reason, and sent to sea;
that many years afterwards he went to Edinburgh to try and see his guardian, with the

result already stated; that he never was married; that he had no friends or relations to the best of his knowledge, and was quite alone in the world. Those who stood to him in the relation of father and mother were the landlord and landlady of the Black Bull, at Wapping, where, ever since a boy, he had put up when on shore; they kept all his money for him when he received his pay, and fed and lodged and looked after him with parental care in return. The rest of his life, he said, he had spent at sea, knocking about in various ships and climates, adding that he had more than once been cast away, and had faced death in many forms.

Such was the man's guileless story. He proved to be the most simple, unselfish, and unsophisticated of human beings. He was told generally why he was wanted, that much depended on him, and how necessary it was he should be ready and at hand when called upon. Yet he never asserted any claim, or made any demand for money as a condition for his acquiescence; he never inquired if any property was at stake, or consulted a lawyer on his own account to see whether terms could be made for him, or showed the slightest disposition to exact or give trouble in any way. He was of course put on a small weekly pension to keep him on shore with his friends at the Black Bull, so that he might be ready when required; but as much time was necessarily consumed in perfecting the legal arrangements before the case could be presented in a complete form to the House of Lords, he even expressed his willingness, old as he was, to go to sea again during the interval, in order that he might not be a burthen on those who were interested in keeping him. "I can't go aloft," he said in proof of his goodwill, "so quick as I used to, but I can haul at the main sheet, or take a turn at the capstan, just as well as ever."

The case of Wilfred Aubrey, soon after the discovery of the sailor, was considered to be complete; and the mass of evidence, documentary and oral, was thereupon duly submitted to a Committee of Privileges of the House of Lords, sitting in the House. Mc-Farlane himself was brought up to London, with difficulty owing to his great age, to be examined. The sailor was present also. No scene in a sensational drama could equal that in the House of Lords when these two men, each with his own separate history, though so nearly allied in blood, were placed side by side at the bar of that tribunal. The aged and decrepid gentleman of four score years and upwards, who hoped that all trace of his early sins had been blotted out, obliterated and forgotten, who had since become respectable " as a householder, and, which is more, as a man that had had losses," who had settled down and established his character as a worthy member of the community, whose daughter had married into one of the proudest and best known families in Yorkshire, thus publicly confronted (so to speak) with his own son— the son whom he had at first for a short time secretly owned, but ever afterwards studiously

disavowed, whom he had not seen for upwards
of forty years, except on that winter's night in
Edinburgh, thirty years before, and then only
for a few moments, of whose existence he was
unaware, and whom now more than ever he
shrunk from acknowledging. On the other
hand, the poor and humble sailor, in his rough
dress, with his weatherbeaten face and horny
hands, standing up, under the roof of that
gorgeous building, surrounded by the pomp
and majesty of the law, the observed of all
observers, then for the first time assured of his
own history, the mystery of his life cleared up,
and brought face to face, after sixty years of
doubt and conjecture, with the author of his
being. The situation was a remarkable one.
" Certainly," as Mrs. Fanny Kemble remarks
in her " Records of Later Life," " novelists
invent nothing more improbable than life ! "

It is not necessary to refer more in detail
to the proceedings before the Committee of
Privileges. Suffice it to say, that after a
happy marshalling of the evidence, all of

which fitted in with great exactitude, the case
of Wilfred Aubrey was pronounced to be
established, and the writ was issued summoning
him to the Upper House as thirteenth Baron
Tutor accordingly.

It may strike the reader as singular that
the House of Lords should, at a time when the
grave might reasonably have closed over the
evidence, try the question of legitimacy and
determine it, which question, upwards of fifty
years previously, whilst the evidence was
fresh, it had refused even to entertain; but
fortunately, during the interval, the rule of
law as to access being presumed when the
husband was " within the four seas " had been
relaxed, and common sense had found a larger
place in our tribunals.

The sailor lived only for a year or two
afterwards. Every Monday morning he walked
from the Black Bull, at Wapping, to the
chambers of the writer at the West End to
receive his weekly pension, and then walked
back with it to place the money in the hands

of his adopted father and mother for safe keeping, he being himself a welcome and unobtru-
sive inmate of the humble attic and sanded
parlour which had formed his only home since
he was of an age to speculate on the mystery
of his life.

SOME SINGULAR WILLS.

SOME SINGULAR WILLS.

PERHAPS there is no period of a man's life when his true nature comes so conspicuously to the front as when he sets himself to the task of arranging the disposition of his property after his death. The ingrained covetousness of one man stands out, strong even in death, when his last testamentary act is so framed as to contain a direction that the money which he leaves behind him shall be accumulated; that no one belonging to him, no one whom he knows, shall enjoy it ; but that, in the course of years, a great heap shall be formed for the eventual benefit of some unborn person or persons, who, on the principle of *omne ignotum*, he fancies will better deserve it than the individuals he does know.

> " How quickly nature falls into revolt
> When gold becomes her object ! "

Fortunately the Legislature has imposed a limit upon such unnatural accumulation.

There are others, again, who are actuated by feelings springing out of something akin to the Romish doctrine of the efficacy of masses for the souls of the departed, and who hope to gain credit for themselves in the next world by bequests to hospitals, dispensaries, and other charities. The human heart is pretty much the same, let the creed be what it may. Their faith in the doctrine may be weak, but it is enough for them to act on the advice of the Presbyterian minister, who, when asked by a Scotch gentleman of fortune on his death-bed whether, if he left a large sum of money to the kirk, it would make his soul safe in the next world, replied, " I would na' just like to be positeeve, but it's weel worth the trying." The human heart of Runjeet Sing nearly lost us the Koh-i-noor. " Runjeet," writes the biographer of Lord Lawrence, " listening on his death-bed to the suggestions of a wily Brahmin, had been half disposed,

like other death-bed penitents, to make his
peace with the other world by sending the
beautiful jewel to adorn the idol of Juggernaut;
but fate reserved it for the ultimate possession
of the English crown." To counteract these
propensities the law again steps in and
declares to be illegal and void all bequests
of land or anything savouring of land for
charitable purposes.

Then we have the proud territorial magnate,
who would, if the law allowed him, tie up his
ancestral mansion and lands to the end of
time. Such men hold on, even after death,
by their lands, "calling them after their own
names," and cherish a scheme for perpetual
entail, which would effectually fetter their
posterity, and prevent the alienation of a
single acre. Vast has been the ingenuity
displayed by conveyancers in constructing
forms to give effect to the motives of family
pride by which persons of this class are
actuated. And it must be admitted that the
feeling is not otherwise than laudable, or, at

the least, that it is excusable. That an
ancestral estate should have been in the uninterrupted possesion of such a family for two,
three, or four hundred years is not an unreasonable foundation for the wish that it
should be handed down and continue in the
same family for as long again. Every year,
however, the tendency of modern legislation
has been more and more to emancipate land
from the views and caprices of the settler,
and more and more opposed to what may be
called a "lock up" of land. The total aboli-
tion of entail, or, at least, the free sale of land
notwithstanding the entail, to which we have
now practically arrived, will interfere with,
and eventually annihilate, the territorial pride
on which entails have hitherto been based.

There is another and smaller class of persons
whose testamentary dispositions seem to be
the result of a kind of craze. They will
bequeath all their property to the Queen, or
to some well-known public character, from
motives which it is impossible to fathom.

More numerous, and more rational, are those who desire to import their own peculiar fancies into their bequests. From such proceed conditions as to residence, compelling the person to whom a house is given to live in it for a stated portion of every year; conditions requiring the legatee to take the name and arms of the donor; conditions of forfeiture in the event of the legatee marrying Mr. or Miss So-and-So, or in case the legatee becomes a Roman Catholic or a Baptist, or a convert to any other persuasion held by the donor to be fatally heterodox; shifting conditions, that is to say, the gift of an estate which is to shift or pass away to somebody else, in the event of the person to whom it is given succeeding to another and different property. Many other fanciful conditions are often proposed, but they seldom see the light, because the professional man consulted at the time pronounces them illegal or incapable of being reduced into form.

Lastly, come a large number of persons who,

some from secretiveness, some from false
economy, prefer making their own wills. Of
these, very few are content to leave their
property in a simple form to any one individual
absolutely, without annexing some sort of
trust, condition, or reservation. Even if they
buy a penny printed form of will at a
stationer's, or follow the precedent given in
Letts's " Diary," they fail to fill it up so as to
give effect to their intentions, or fail perhaps
to satisfy the requirements of the Wills Act
as to signature and attestation. Such persons
are the lawyer's best friends. A fruitful
harvest of litigation has been gathered from
home-made wills, and there is a plentiful crop
still ripening for the sickle.

As regards signature and attestation, it may
be observed, by way of parenthesis, that it
certainly was a glaring anomaly that, prior to
the passing of the Wills Act in 1838, a freeholder or yeoman possessing only an acre of
land could not leave it by will unless that will
were signed by him and attested by three

witnesses, whereas a Coutts or a Rothschild might bequeath millions of money by a few lines scribbled by himself on a sheet of note-paper, or on the back of an envelope, or (as once actually happened) on the flyleaf of a cookery-book, without any witness at all.

The professional man advising all the fore-going classes of persons (except the last), should consider it within his province to control the whims and caprices of his client, to endeavour to direct the property into its natural channel, to simplify the bequests, and to throw the weight of his authority against irritating conditions and unreasonable techni-calities. At no time is the influence of the solicitor more valuable. Nor is the advice he gives at that time the less honourable and meritorious because it can only be known to himself; and however sound the advice and however beneficial its consequences, no reward follows to him, except that of his own con-science.

As a rule, the large number of wills which

every year are proved and acted upon, without attracting notice or comment, certainly are due to the intentions of the testator being honestly conceived, and controlled and put into form under good advice.

It is impossible, however, for any solicitor engaged in large practice not to come in contact occasionally with instances of strange wills and strange complications arising from them, some of which, from their exceptional nature, may safely enlist the attention of the general reader. Of these, the following are a few which have come under the direct professional experience of the writer:—

Lord Armadale was possessed of extensive family estates in the Western Highlands of Scotland, which estates were strictly entailed on his eldest son, and so on, in the male line, in succession, according to the Scotch law, which, at the time of which we speak, admitted of a perpetual entail. He married an English lady, by whom he had a son born before the marriage, and a son and several other children born subsequently to the marriage. All these children were brought up together as one family, living in the same home, bearing the same family name, without distinction; and none of the children were aware, till they were of mature age, of the line of demarcation which was supposed to separate the status of the eldest son from that of the others. The fact, of course, was known to the elder relatives of the family, one of whom, a Yorkshire squire, possessing a valuable estate in the county, entirely at his own disposal, having no children of his own, and commiserating the position of his nephew, the eldest son, the more so because the son himself was ignorant of it, made a will, and by it bequeathed the Yorkshire estate to the eldest son by name absolutely. The uncle's intention was thereby to make up, in some degree, for the severe disappointment which would befall the eldest son when his true position was made known to him.

But as Lord Armadale was of Scotch origin,
and as there might, after all, be a doubt
whether his subsequent marriage did not
legitimate the eldest son, though born before
the marriage, the Yorkshire uncle added a
codicil to his will, carrying in itself the germs
of litigation, declaring that if the eldest son
should at any time succeed to the Scotch
Highland estates, then the Yorkshire estate
should shift from him and pass to his next
brother. His object was to prevent the
possibility of the eldest son, born before the
marriage, enjoying both estates to the detriment of the eldest son born after the marriage.
The law of England and of Scotland differ as
to the effect of marriage on the issue born
previously. The Scotch law legitimates the
issue born before the marriage. Not so the
English law.

Lord Armadale died, and was followed very
shortly by the Yorkshire uncle. On the deaths
of these two the facts became generally
known, and the relative position of the two

sons, the one born before the marriage and the other afterwards, seems to have been determined as a matter of course and without any question. The eldest son accepted his status as illegitimate, and under his uncle's will took possession of the Yorkshire estate, married and settled down there as a useful English country gentleman, duly estimated by the neighbours, and held by them in much respect. The second son, at the same time, assumed the title, and inherited the Scotch Highland estates, becoming a kilted chieftain, the head of his clan, lord of a deer forest, of grouse moors, lochs, and salmon rivers. The position of the two brothers could not possibly have been more contrasted, and both were satisfied.

Matters continued undisturbed on this footing for ten or twelve years, during which time the young Lord Armadale had been following in the groove of many other Highland proprietors, and had been living at a rate far beyond his means. He had, in fact, become

heavily involved in debt. His creditors, finding that they had but slender chance of payment out of a life estate, or life rent as it is
termed in Scotland, which was all the young
lord possessed, and that the Highland estates,
being strictly entailed, could not be sold for
their benefit, began to turn their attention to
the shifting clause in the codicil to the Yorkshire uncle's will. "If," they argued, "we
can establish the fact that the eldest son has
been legitimated by the subsequent marriage
of his parents, he must then succeed to the
entailed Highland estates, whereupon the
Yorkshire estate will, under the terms of
the codicil, shift from him and pass on to the
young lord absolutely. We shall then be able
to sell every acre of the Yorkshire estate, and
by that means be paid in full."

It was not a bad move from their point of
view. The net rental of each of the two
estates was about the same, namely £8000 a
year; but the Yorkshire was a fee simple,
the Scotch a mere life rent, and therefore

there was no comparison between the selling value of the respective interests of the two brothers in the two estates.

Accordingly, they put pressure on the young lord to commence proceedings in England against his elder brother, with the object of claiming possession of the Yorkshire estate under the shifting clause.

Then was presented the strange and unnatural spectacle of two brothers engaged in a formidable litigation between themselves, the elder brother insisting on maintaining his status of illegitimacy to which he had submitted for so many years, and contending strenuously against any proof of his legitimacy, by which contention alone could he defend his title to the Yorkshire estate.

The whole question turned on the domicile of the late Lord Armadale. If he were originally a domiciled Scotchman, and had never lost his domicile of origin, then the Scotch law would apply; but if he had abandoned his domicile of origin and had acquired an English domicile, then the facts would be governed by the English law.

The question of domicile is one of fact and intention. He was born in Scotland, no doubt, and of Scotch parents, but he was educated at Eton. From Eton he entered the army and served with an English regiment in various parts of the globe. On leaving the army he married an Englishwoman, bought a house in London, and brought up his children at schools in England. Other acts he did, not necessary to be here detailed, from which it might be inferred that he had chosen England as the place of his abode, and never had any intention of returning permanently to Scotland.

That, at all events, was the view insisted upon by the elder brother, who had no wish, on compulsion, to alter the whole course of his life, who had become attached to his Yorkshire property, and who firmly resolved not to surrender it, except on the verdict of a Yorkshire jury. Underlying these reasons there might be detected a morbid feeling which led him to despise, and even discountenance, any effort to efface the social obliquy under which he had suffered for so many years, and for which he could attribute no blame to himself. If the right to the peerage had certainly followed the result it might possibly have been some temptation to him to yield; but, strange to say, although everything else was either Scotch or English, the peerage itself was of Irish creation, and it by no means followed that a Scotch legitimacy would carry with it the Irish title.

And so the litigation was carried on. A Commission was issued into Scotland, which was attended by the writer, and which sat for many weeks in Edinburgh and other places, and every minute fact in the life of the parents was inquired into likely to bear on the question whether the late Lord Armadale intended to live and die a Scotchman or an Englishman.

The creditors of the young lord, when they launched the proceedings, were scarcely aware of the ponderous nature of the stone they had set rolling. There are some things in this world, which, once set a going, it is not easy to stop. A law suit is one of them. They became alarmed at the enormous cost of the proceedings. Who was to bear the cost? Where was the money to come from in case of failure? They hesitated, but could not stop; it was too late to hold back the swelling tide of litigation, for the titles to both estates had been blown upon and neither property was now negotiable. In this predicament, it was at length happily suggested that the brothers should apply in concert for an Act of Parliament to quiet both the titles on the footing of the subsisting possession, the elder brother remaining in Yorkshire and the younger in Scotland. The Act was accordingly drafted and submitted to the late Lord Shaftesbury, then chairman of Committees of the House of Lords, the dread Cerberus guarding the portal through which all measures of the kind must pass before they can become law. He was startled at the boldness of the experiment, and protested, in language which none could use more forcibly, and which could scarcely without profanity be repeated, that it was impossible to withdraw the case from the ordinary tribunals of the country. However, the family had many influential friends, political and otherwise, and it is not necessary to say more than that Lord Shaftesbury's objections were eventually overcome, and the Act passed which terminated the litigation on the footing of the subsisting possession. The elder brother remained undisturbed in Yorkshire, and the younger in Scotland, whilst the creditors of the latter reaped no benefit from their ill-advised move, except to add to the debt on the Scotch estates by the costs of the litigation.

Life Insurance Companies have become more cautious of late years in the character of the risks which they accept. There is a growing tendency on the part of all respectable

companies to treat every policy, when once
accepted, as indisputable, that is, never to
dispute payment afterwards under any circumstances. Exercising caution in the first
instance, they are enabled to act with corresponding liberality afterwards, and in so doing
they best consult their own interest, for if an
Insurance Company earns a name for being
contentious the public will wisely avoid it.

Before this principle was so generally recognized as it is now, one John Goslett, who had
been a subaltern in a line regiment, but had
retired, and was enrolled in one of the veteran
battalions, insured his life in a London Insurance office for £1500. He sent in his proposal and medical certificates as a perfectly
sound healthy life, and the proposal was
accepted and the premium assessed at the
ordinary rate for a healthy life. He lived
many years afterwards, and on his death his
executors produced the probate of his will to
the office as proof of their title to receive the
sum assured. The will itself on such occasions

is seldom or ever read. There is no necessity
for it; the office contents itself with looking at
the mere Probate Act annexed to the will to
see who are the executors. However, on the
present occasion, the secretary chanced to
cast his eye over the will, and there found an
elaborate reason given by Goslett for effecting
the insurance. The reason alleged was his
shattered health owing to fever contracted in
the tropics whilst on military service, and his
continued suffering which made his life more
than ordinarily precarious. Apprehension of
early death, he said, and anxiety for his family
had induced him to make provision for them
by means of the insurance. The directors of
the office with which the policy had been
effected thereupon considered that something
like a fraud had been practised upon them,
and were inclined to dispute the policy altogether; but having regard to the fact that
Goslett had lived for many years, notwithstanding his prediction of an early death, they
offered formally to pay the executors the whole

sum assured, less such a sum as Goslett would
have paid, in the shape of increased premium,
had the true facts been disclosed at the time.
It was a fair offer, but it was refused; and,
relying on the sympathies of a jury, an action
was brought by the executors against the
company. The cause was actually carried to
trial at the Assizes at Croydon; but the presiding judge, when told of the offer, would not
allow the case to go to the jury, and insisted
on the executors accepting the offer. The
company, as an act of grace, at the suggestion
of the judge, bore their own costs of the proceedings. They would have done more wisely,
and the cost to them would have been less if
they had paid the whole money in the first
instance without objection.

Sir William Hall had (it is not necessary to
specify the precise time when) contracted to
purchase from Dr. Bisham a landed estate in
Gloucestershire, for £60,000. The title to the

estate had been satisfactorily deduced in the ordinary way down to and including the will of his brother, under which Dr. Bisham acquired the property. The terms of this will were simple enough. It gave the property to Dr. Bisham and his heirs, such being the most comprehensive words that can be used for giving a property out and out. The purchase was on the eve of completion, when an anonymous letter was received by Sir William Hall, advising him, before completing the purchase, to inspect the original will at Doctors' Commons.

The original will was accordingly immediately inspected, when, strange to say, it was found that the words " and his heirs " had been struck through with a pen. The other part of the gift remained intact, which then read as a gift of the estate to Dr. Bisham. Now, the probate copy of the will issued from the Prerogative Office, which had been produced in evidence of the title had quoted the words as a gift to " Dr. Bisham and his heirs,"

and on looking further for an explanation of
this discrepancy there was found annexed to
the original will an affidavit by Dr. Bisham
himself, stating that his brother shortly before
his death had sent for him (Dr. Bisham), and
desired him to read the will to see that his
(the brother's) intention to leave him the
Gloucestershire property out and out had been
carried into effect; that he (Dr. Bisham) read
the will there and then, and erroneously sup-
posing that the words "and his heirs" created
an entail, he, in his brother's presence, took a
pen and himself scratched out those words.
On this affidavit it appeared that the registrar
of the Prerogative Office had restored the words
"and his heirs" in the probate copy, without
referring in any way to the affidavit. As the
probate copy of the will alone had been produced in evidence of the title, there was no
reason to suspect that there was anything
amiss or that the gift of the estate was otherwise than a gift out and out.

However, there was quite enough here to

induce Sir William Hall to pause. The funds
wherewith to pay for the estate were in court
and the title therefore required to be approved
by the court before the purchase could be
completed. It was in the days of the old
masters in Chancery, and the master in rotation to whom it had been referred by the court
to approve of the title was Mr. Lynch, one of
Daniel O'Connell's tail, who had been appointed
to that snug and enviable berth, not, it was
said, so much for his knowledge of law as
through the influence, or, it would be nearer
the truth to write, at the dictation, of the
great agitator. The meeting at which the
novel discovery was to be submitted to the
master was attended by all the parties concerned, and most opportunely, but quite accidentally, Mr. Preston, the renowned conveyancer, happened to be in the master's room at
the time, talking to him on some other matter
of business.

Very few are now alive who can remember
Mr. Preston. He was known half a century

ago as the leading conveyancer of the time.
His publications were then the standard works
on the law of real property, now, owing to the
tide of law amendment having set in so rapidly
of late years, they are left high and dry on the
shelves of the lawyer's library. In person
he was the embodiment of all the technicalities of conveyancing; attenuated, bloodless,
wrinkled, with a skin the colour of kindred
parchment; in character, tenacious, conscious
of his own learning and ever ready to dis-
play it.

"Look at Preston," said a legal wit, seated
on the back benches of the Court, with no
brief to occupy his attention. "Look at
him; he always reminds me of a tenant in
tail with possibility of issue extinct." A professional joke for which an apology is due to
the general reader.

However, at the meeting referred to Mr.
Preston was present, and remained in the
room whilst the facts were stated to the
master.

"Here, Mr. Preston," said Master Lynch, with a mellow Galway brogue, "here is a point which you can decide better than I can. What say you?"

"Nothing in it," replied Mr. Preston, slowly and with great authority,—"nothing whatever in it. By the recent Act, a gift to a man without any words of inheritance is a gift to him absolutely. Here is a gift to Dr. Bisham, and that is sufficient to give him the property out and out."

"Pardon me for a moment," said the writer, acting as solicitor for Sir William Hall. "The Act says that such a gift shall be good, *unless a contrary intention shall appear*. From the fact of the words *and his heirs* having been originally written and afterwards struck out, it must be inferred that the testator had altered his intention, and did not intend to give his brother an estate of inheritance, but an estate for his life only; for Dr. Bisham's own affidavit, unsupported, cannot be admitted as reliable evidence in his own interest."

Mr. Preston was silent. He looked at the speaker over his spectacles for a few moments, and then replied, "Right; the testator's heir-at-law must join to perfect the title."

And Dr. Bisham had to procure the concurrence of the testator's heir-at-law (a collateral relative), at some expense and much inconvenience, before his title to the estate could be perfected. Thereupon the purchase was completed.

It may not be beside the question to call attention to the personal risks which solicitors run on occasions of this kind. The probate copy of a will under the seal in those days of the Prerogative Office, and now of the Court of Probate, is invariably accepted as sufficient evidence of the contents of the will itself. Yet the probate was not then, at law, considered evidence when real property was considered. It was clearly the duty of the solicitor to inspect the original will itself, and in this case, but for the anonymous letter, the solicitor for Sir William Hall might have been personally liable for the £60,000 had the testator's heir-at-law refused to concur, and had he ousted the purchaser on the ground that the gift of the Gloucestershire estate to Dr. Bisham was a gift for his life only.

———

Sir Graham West was an elderly baronet of eccentric habits, possessed of an old family estate in one of the southern counties and considerable personal property besides. He was married, but had no children. During the latter years of his life he had a fancy to amuse himself by making his will. He therefore bought a parchment-covered book, containing a hundred blank pages, or thereabouts, signed his name on the first page of the book, and called in three persons to witness his signature. These persons wrote their names on the first page also, just beneath his own signature, and he in his turn attested their signatures.

Having heard that three witnesses were

necessary to a will of landed property, he
thought he had thus complied strictly with
the requirements of the law, and that he
might then proceed to write what he liked
at his leisure in the remainder of the book.
Accordingly, he occupied himself at intervals
by writing a page or two of his will at a time
just as his fancy took him, beginning with a
note pasted inside the cover to state that the
pencil entries should · be regarded as equally
valid with the ink entries.

His leading idea was to tie up his family
estate as strictly as possible, and to add more
land to the existing territory. Though he
had a smattering of law terms, he was by no
means sure what the legal effect of the phraseology at his command would be. Therefore,
to obtain a moral, as well as a legal, hold on
the persons whom he intended to benefit, he
began his will by " holding up to the direst
execration and infamy any person who should
endeavour to alter or overset by suffering a
recovery by any Act of Parliament, or by any

other means whatever, the provisions of that his will."

Poor man! If he could have risen from the grave and listened to the fun made of his exordium in court, when the will came to be litigated, by the lawyers whose aid he despised in his lifetime, and who took their revenge upon him afterwards by ridiculing his anathema and by disputing every line of his dispositions, he would have been horrified indeed.

Having, as he thought, protected himself by this awful denunciation, he proceeded to give the income of all his property to his wife for her life. Then, within eighteen months after his wife's death, he directed that all his Bank of England and other stock, and all his money, should be laid out in the purchase of land. If the land were not purchased by the first taker within the eighteen months, then the gift to him would be forfeited, and the next taker would come in and have the same period to make the purchase, with the like condition of forfeiture, and so on through a long string of successive takers.

Then came the list of persons who were to take both the old family estate and the purchased land under the entail, and this was the most curious part of the will. They were represented by letters of the alphabet! The first to take was called L, the second M, the third N, and so on down to Z, with the addition, after each letter, of words of entail in favour of the male issue of each. With the exception of these letters of the alphabet, all the will was written in ink, but these letters were written in pencil, so that if the testator thought fit, or if any one letter of the alphabet should happen to offend him, he might rub out that letter with india-rubber and substitute another letter in its place. That clever contrivance, he thought, would save him the trouble of rewriting the whole of his will, should he change his intention, or even of adding a codicil.

But who was to interpret these ciphers?

Quite at the end of the parchment-covered book there was a note as follows :—" The key to this my will is written on a card which will be found in the drawer of my wooden writing-desk in my library." And true enough when the death happened there the card was found, about the size of an ordinary playing-card, with the column of letters interpreted as follows :—

" L means Sebastian John West;
M means Hugh Thomas West;"

and so on through the remainder of the alphabet. The persons designated were quite young men, mostly great-nephews of the testator, the first taker, L, being the eldest son of a younger nephew, the second taker, M, being the second son of his eldest nephew, the subsequent letters being other collateral relatives. All these names, too, on the card were written in pencil, and could in like manner be rubbed out with india-rubber at pleasure, and other names substituted.

The entail down to the last letter of the alphabet was strictly enjoined. It was the

great effort of the will. The remainder of
the parchment-covered book contained what
might be called fancy-work, namely, a sketch
of the crest and coat-of-arms each taker was
to bear, under the penalty of forfeiture; directions as to the testator's manner of interment;
as to the hatchment to be placed in the
chancel of the parish church "with ring and
hook;" the names of the pall-bearers; the size
and material of coffin, which was to be "of
cedar, lined top, bottom, and sides with Russia
leather, and embellished with armorial and
funeral devices richly; camphor and spices to
be put into the cedar coffin as much as possible; the funeral procession to be dignified
and conducted with banners," etc. Then
there was the gift of an annuity to one Martha
Hack, to enable her to provide for his parrot—
and a question here arose whether the annuity
was for the life of Martha or for the life of
the parrot; directions respecting a new cage
for his parrot every two years; directions
respecting his favourite horses, all of which

were to have " a run for life, with plenty of
chaff and bran, and warm sheds during the
winter;" directions respecting the building
and endowment of almshouses, and the
stipend of the apothecary and of the steward
in charge. "The requisites for a steward
were to be a character for cleanliness and
civility, and a knowledge of reading, writing,
and arithmetic in a common way; he was to
read the Litany on certain days in an audible
voice, and previously to ring the chapel bell."
Then followed directions as to the number of
the poor persons to inhabit the almshouses,
their pocket-money, dress, meals, and obser-
vances. In short, the rest of the book was
filled up with eccentric directions on all
manner of miscellaneous subjects.

Here was a grand home-made will for the
lawyers ! with plenty of money to furnish the
sinews of war, for the Bank of England stock
alone at the time of the testator's death
amounted to upwards of £95,000 stock, equal
to about £250,000 sterling.

Regardless of the poor man's anathema, the
battle began the moment the breath was out
of his body. The widow boldly and at once
contended that the whole will was "a farrago
of nonsense" and void for uncertainty, knowing full well that if the will were declared void
she would take one half of all the personalty,
as in the case of an intestacy. She failed,
however, in that contention. The will, having
come into operation prior to the Wills Act,
was considered capable of being construed,
and was, together with the card, held to be
good; for, as has been before pointed out, no
witnesses were necessary at that time to a
will of money or personalty, however large
the amount. It was held void as to the
family landed estate, because, though attested
by three witnesses, they signed their names
before the will, and not after it. And it was
held void also as to the almshouses, as being
contrary to the Mortmain Acts.

Directly after the death of the widow, a
scramble ensued for investing the bank stock

and money in the purchase of land. Estates had to be found and purchased within the eighteen months, and concurrently the question was raised, and strenuously fought, whether L or M was the first taker, for portions of the will were so ambiguously worded and so contradictory, as to leave that most important question in doubt. However, L was judicially declared to be the winning horse; but no sooner was that primary question decided than another followed, namely, whether he was entitled to an estate for his life only or to an estate of inheritance. M fought this question also, equally strenuously, because if L took an estate for life only, and died without issue, M would come next. It was carried up to the House of Lords, who decided that L took an estate for life only; but the decision turned out to be of no practical consequence, for L and his eldest son afterwards, on the very day on which the latter came of age, notwithstanding the anathema, barred the entail, and so acquired the purchased

estates absolutely, completely cutting out
both M and all the subsequent letters of the
alphabet.

Thus man proposes and the law disposes!
The will, however, is a good example of the
various eccentricities of will-makers gathered
into one focus. For here we have the desire
to aggrandise and to postpone the enjoyment
of the intended benefit to a remoter and less
known generation; the craving to tie up the
land; the credit sought to be opened in the
next world by a gift to charitable uses, and
the secretiveness and parsimony of the will-
maker—all fortunately restricted and controlled by the wisdom of the Legislature.

A little unpleasant episode arose out of the
foregoing circumstances which deserves to be
mentioned. L and M were first cousins, and
both were, at the same period, lieutenants in
separate regiments of the Household Cavalry.
Just after the judicial decision which gave L
the first life estate in the purchased property,
he received two or three anonymous letters,

written in the Roman character so as to dis-
guise the handwriting, warning him that
unless he made immediate and ample provision for his cousin, who, as the letters alleged,
had been defrauded of his rights by an unjust
litigation, his (L's) life would be taken. He
might employ every precaution (the letters
stated) to protect himself, it would be of no
avail. If he did not act justly by his cousin
he would certainly be destroyed. Suspicion
attached to the cousin himself as being the
author of these letters, and on comparing
them with his acknowledged letters it was
found that the postage stamps on all, that is
on the anonymous as well as on the acknowledged letters, had been affixed diamond ways,
with the angle of the stamp upwards ; the
watermark on the paper was the same ; and
there were some other trifling coincidences,
all of which tended to confirm the suspicion.
What was to be done ? Either to take no
notice whatever of the anonymous letters, or
to act vigorously on the suspicion and hazard

the consequences. The latter course was
adopted. A warrant was applied for at Bow
Street against M, and was granted. He was
summarily arrested at his lodgings in London,
and carried off to the lock-up house. His rooms
were then searched, and, together with loaded
revolvers and other formidable weapons, there
were found in the blotting-book on his writing-
table scraps of paper on which he had been
practising the very Roman character in which
the anonymous letters were written, and some
of the very words. There was no resisting
this evidence. An appeal was made *ad miseri-
cordiam* to L, and, on an ample admission and
apology in writing, M was discharged after a
few days' incarceration, having gained an
experience which to a Life Guardsman must,
at all events, have had the merit of novelty.

The lives of men in a high social position
may be said, within certain limits, to be the
property of the public. Such men move under

a subdued form of the same fierce light which beats upon the throne, and in this country, more than in any other, are they as a class looked up to, admired, and respected. But to whom much has been given of them shall much be required, and it is doubly their own fault, doubly to be deplored, if instead of setting their lighted candle upon a candlestick they themselves perversely hide it under a bushel. In the case about to be mentioned it is not proposed to transgress those limits, but as the facts of the case have already been presented to the public in detached portions, and have received the sanction of judicial notice, they are, in a sense, matter for comment in a work of this kind. Avoiding the very suspicion of scandal or gossip, no further details will now be given than such as the curious could by inquiry and research collect for themselves or such as they are reasonably entitled to know.

Richard Seymour, fourth Marquis of Hertford, as will be seen by the peerage, was born

in 1800, the son of Francis, third Marquis, by
his marriage with Maria Fagniani, an Italian
singer. Together with the title, the fourth
Marquis inherited, on his father's death, the
family possessions, which consisted of two
princely estates in England, namely, Ragley
in Warwickshire, and Sudbourn in Suffolk,
and in addition a still larger landed estate in
the county of Antrim, without its equal in
Ireland for order, fertility, compactness, and
the well-to-do character of its tenantry. He
inherited also from his father a very large
fortune in personalty.

But he was not induced by these possessions
to reside either in England or in Ireland, for
English country life had no attraction for him,
still less was he tempted by the position of a
resident Irish landlord. Nor did he act as if
the ownership of such vast possessions carried
with it any corresponding duties. He remained a bachelor, and though well fitted for
public as well as private life by reason of his
acquirements, cultivated tastes, manners, and

conversational powers, he shunned his country
and the society of his countrymen, and pre-
ferred Paris and the Parisians. There, partly
at his house in the Rue Lafitte, and partly at
his villa, Bagatelle, in the Bois de Boulogne,
he passed all the last years of his life, content-
ing himself with seeing occasionally a very few
only of his intimate friends, with adding largely
to his investments in houses in that improving
capital, and in foreign funds, and amusing
himself by purchasing objects of art. In the
selection of these objects his knowledge, taste,
and unlimited wealth gave him an advantage
over most other competitors, though some of
them were royal personages and representatives of great national collections, but who
nevertheless often bid against him in vain for
the coveted object.

The value of the unequalled private collection thus formed was appreciated by the public
when, not long since, it was exhibited in the
building erected for the purpose at Bethnal
Green.

His younger brother, known as Lord Henry Seymour, was his heir presumptive, that is, if the heirship had been free from question. But there was a strange question, and one of notoriety, affecting the status of the younger brother.

Francis, third Marquis, was travelling in France in May, 1803, when the English Ambassador at the Tuileries, Lord Whitworth, having received his passports from the First Consul, the British Government promulgated a declaration of war against France, and as a matter of course issued letters of marque. Buonaparte, within a week after the declaration, and in defiance of all hitherto known rules, retaliated by summarily arresting all British subjects then in France, many of whom had been tempted, after the Peace of Amiens, to travel on the continent in search of health, amusement, or business. Some of these prisoners, and amongst them the marquis, were sent to the Fortress of Verdun, and there detained, being afterwards commonly

known as *détenus*, and but few of them re-
gained their liberty till the downfall of
Buonaparte in 1814. Meanwhile, the mar-
chioness remained in England, and during that
period gave birth to a son, Lord Henry, under
circumstances which cast a doubt as to his
right of succession. His elder brother, the
fourth Marquis, out of respect for his mother,
never admitted the doubt, but always recognized his brother as his rightful heir. Happily,
however, so far as it concerns the question
just referred to, Lord Henry died in his
brother's lifetime, without ever having been
married, so that the point never came up for
adjudication.

On Lord Henry's death, Admiral Sir George
Seymour, who was the eldest son of the next
brother of the second Marquis, and consequently first cousin once removed to the
fourth Marquis, became heir presumptive to
the latter. The admiral was as noble, right-
minded, and independent a man as ever
breathed. Having formed his own opinion as

to the status of Lord Henry, he made no
secret of it, though had he consulted his own
interests he might doubtless have conciliated
his cousin the marquis by acknowledging
Lord Henry, and thereby possibly have reaped
some temporal advantage.

As the event proved, however, the admiral
was not personally affected either way by the
opinion which he held, for he also died in the
lifetime of.his cousin the marquis.

In the month of August, 1870, the marquis
himself died at his house in the Rue Lafitte,
at the age of seventy. The preparations for
his funeral were hasty, and attended with
distracting interest, for the populace filled the
streets, wild with excitement at the approach of
the victorious German Army, already swarming
outside the fortifications to invest the city.
The mourners, as they stood round the open
grave in Père la Chaise, actually

> " Heard the distant and random gun,
>   That the foe was sullenly firing."

On the return of the mourners through the

crowded streets to the house, the repositories of the deceased marquis were rapidly searched, some of those friends who had followed the remains being anxious to leave Paris before their exit was finally barred by the complete investment of the city.

Several separate testamentary papers were found, all of which have since been proved and can be seen and inspected by the curious at the principal registry of the Court of Probate in London, on payment of a shilling. Of these testamentary papers two only need be specified, as the others are foreign to the present purpose. One was a voluminous will, dated in June, 1838, prior to the death of Lord Henry Seymour, carefully prepared under the best professional advice, and purporting to be a settlement of the Antrim estates on Lord Henry Seymour for his life, and on his issue, and on failure of that line upon Sir Hamilton Seymour for his life, with remainder to his first and other sons successively in strict order of entail, with powers of jointuring and raising portions for younger children, and all other provisions commonly inserted in strict settlements of the kind, followed by a gift by the marquis of the residue of his personal estate to Lord Henry Seymour absolutely. The will contained no devise of the residuary reality. The other testamentary paper was a holograph codicil, dated the 7th June, 1850, in the following words :—

"This is a further codicil to the last will of me, Richard Seymour, Marquis of Hertford, which bears date on or about the 21st day of June, 1838. I hereby revoke the bequest contained in my will of the residue of all my real and personal estates to my brother, Lord Henry Seymour, and to reward as much as I can Richard Wallace, for all his care and attention to my dear mother, and likewise for his devotion to me during a long and painful illness I had in Paris in 1840, and on all other occasions,—I give such residue to the said Richard Wallace, now living at the Hotel des Bains, Boulogne-sur-Mer, in France, and whose

domicile, previous to the revolution of February, 1848, was in my mother's house, Rue
Taitbout No. 3, Paris, absolutely."

Lord Henry Seymour was at this date still
living, but he was, as the marquis well knew,
a very wealthy man independently. He died
unmarried in 1859, bequeathing his wealth, as
will be remembered, to the hospitals of Paris
and London, and no question arose in his
interests either upon the will or codicil.

Shortly after the conclusion of the Franco-
German war, Richard Wallace, the beneficiary
under the codicil, was created a baronet, in
recognition of his munificence towards English
residents and others during the great siege
which followed immediately on the marquis's
death, and he is now Sir Richard Wallace,
M.P. for the county of Antrim.

Upon these two testamentary documents a
question of vital importance arose between Sir
Hamilton Seymour and Sir Richard Wallace.
Ragley and Sudbourn did not come into discussion. The marquis had no power of dispo-

sition over those estates, which passed, without dispute, under old family settlements, together with the title, to Colonel Francis Hugh Seymour, the eldest son of the admiral. But with regard to the Antrim estates, over which the marquis had the absolute power of disposal, the question was, Did the codicil revoke the devise contained in the will of those estates to Sir Hamilton Seymour and his sons, and give everything to Sir Richard Wallace? It was a question worth fighting about, as the rental of the Antrim estates approached £60,000 a year, but the antagonists were not evenly matched so far as the sinews of war were concerned. Sir Richard Wallace had indisputably, under the codicil, come into the whole of the personalty (including the art treasures), the value and amount of which it would be difficult to exaggerate; whereas Sir Hamilton had inherited from his father the portion only of a younger son, to which fell to be added such sums as he might have laid by during his long and meritorious career as a diplomatist.

He was the son of another younger brother
of the second Marquis, and consequently a first
cousin once removed of the testator, the
fourth Marquis, in the same degree of relation-
ship as the admiral, only that the latter was
the son of an elder brother. Sir Hamilton
had a European reputation. He had filled the
post of Ambassador for Great Britain at
Brussels, Lisbon, Vienna, and lastly at St.
Petersburg, where he was serving at the
breaking out of the Crimean war. His graphic
letters from St. Petersburg to the Foreign
Office, recounting his conversations with the
Emperor Nicholas, just before the war, and
how the Czar proposed to treat the "sick
man," will be indelible in history. A more
accomplished gentleman than Sir Hamilton
could rarely be met with. His long residence
at the principal courts of Europe had furnished
him with an experience of no ordinary kind.
Of this he had abundantly availed himself, and
those who, like the writer, had the privilege of
his acquaintance will value his memory at its

full worth, and remember with delight his sparkling anecdotes and brilliant conversation, drawn from the rich store which he had accumulated during his long and varied life.

Accustomed to the society which is supposed to be enjoyed at its best in courts and capitals, a new phase of existence was now unexpectedly opened to him by the gift to him, under the will, of the Antrim estates.   It was late in the day for him to change the whole course of his life, from a diplomatist and a man of society to an Irish landlord; but the magnitude of the stake cast into shade all considerations of personal predilection and convenience.

Acting under the advice of the most eminent counsel in Dublin, he assumed his rights to be unaffected by the codicil, and crossing over to Ireland took possession of the estates. The writer accompanied him on that occasion. They were received and acknowledged by the resident agent of the late marquis, who introduced Sir Hamilton to many of the tenants as their future landlord. With mixed feelings did

Sir Hamilton go through this unavoidable duty, and as he traversed the main road intersecting the estates, and looked to the right and left of him, over an uninteresting country, from Lisburn to Lough Neagh, peopled for miles and miles by tenant farmers, he could not conceal the doubt which pressed upon him whether he should ever be able to reconcile his new duties as a resident Irish landlord, for resident he felt he must be, with his previous habits, tastes, and inclinations.

The initiative thus taken by Sir Hamilton was promptly responded to by Sir Richard Wallace, who thereupon commenced proceedings at law in Ireland, which resulted in a formal submission to the full Court of Common Pleas in Dublin of the legal question, whether the codicil revoked the will; in other words, whether Sir Hamilton or Sir Richard was entitled to the Antrim estates.

The legal question was elaborately argued before the four judges of the Court of Common Pleas, all lawyers of reputation, enjoying the

confidence of the public. The foremost
counsel of the Irish Bar were engaged on
each side, and the arguments lasted several
days, at the end of which judgment was
reserved.

After an interval of some six or eight
weeks, it was announced that judgment would
be delivered on a stated day. The writer
was present on the appointed day, as he was
during the argument. No sort of inkling had
transpired of the view which would probably
be taken by the four judges, whether they
favoured one side or the other, whether they
would be unanimous or divided in opinion;
but if unanimous, the practice of the court
was for the junior judge first to deliver his
judgment.

Silence reigned in the crowded court on the
appointed morning (for the case had excited
great public interest) as the four judges filed
in and took their seats on the bench. Were
they unanimous, or were they not? The
junior judge first opened his mouth. Evi-

dently the court was unanimous—but on
which side ? He recapitulated the documents
and facts with a tantalizing deliberation; but
as he proceeded the mists gradually lifted,
and his reasoning showed that the judgment
of all the four judges would be unanimously
in support of the will against the codicil, and
that Sir Hamilton was entitled, under it, to
the Antrim estates.

And so it proved. Nothing daunted, Sir
Richard Wallace appealed from the Common
Pleas decision to the Appellate Court, ordinarily composed of the four judges of the
Court of Queen's Bench and the four of the
Court of Exchequer; but as one of the counsel
in the previous argument had since been
made a judge of the Court of Queen's Bench,
he would not sit to hear the appeal, which
was consequently heard before the seven
remaining judges.

All the former arguments were repeated in
the Appellate Court, and again the judgment
was reserved. Mark the glorious uncertainty

of the law! When judgment was pronounced
on the appeal, four out of the seven judges
declared their opinion to be in favour of Sir
Richard Wallace and three in favour of Sir
Hamilton, the effect of the judgment of the
majority on the appeal being to reverse the
unanimous decision of the four judges of
the Court of Common Pleas. A strange
anomaly in our judicial system, that though
seven judges, namely, four of the Court of
Common Pleas, and three of the Appellate
Court, should be in favour of Sir Hamilton,
yet that the minority of four in the aggregate
of eleven judges, all belonging to courts of
co-ordinate jurisdiction, should be able to
reverse the decision of the seven !

However, such was the law, and there was
no use to declaim or contend against it. Sir
Hamilton had now no alternative but in his
turn to appeal to the House of Lords. Cir-
cumstanced as he was, with limited means
and a large family, he felt he was not justified
in incurring the risk of another possible defeat.

Overtures for a compromise were commenced, to which he leant with more readiness in proportion as his disinclination increased to alter the whole course of his life and pass his remaining days in Ireland, and it was ultimately arranged that possession of the Antrim estates should be made over to Sir Richard Wallace on payment by him of a large sum of money, which was to be settled on Sir Hamilton and his eldest and other sons, in like manner as the estates would have been had he retained them.

Having regard to what has since occurred in Ireland, and to the present condition of that misguided country, perhaps the recipients of the money may now be considered, from every point of view, to have had the best of the bargain.

With some hesitation, lest the motive might be misconstrued, the following trait in Sir Hamilton's character is added. One day, pending the litigation, but before any decision on it had been pronounced, he was seen getting out of a four-wheeled cab, drawn up at the door of the writer's chambers, carrying under his arm a large brown-paper parcel. He walked with it upstairs, and addressing the writer, as he entered the room and untied the string, said, " See, I have brought you, before we know what's going to happen in court, a small mark of my appreciation of your services. You'll value it more as coming from me whilst I am a poor man. If I succeed and become rich there is no merit in giving such things." The parcel contained a handsome silver salver with an appropriate inscription.

MASTER AND MAN.

MASTER AND MAN.

THERE stands on the banks of the Thames a prominent house, well known to those who frequent the river. It is not far from London, and yet, by reason of its distance from a railway station, has not been brought into immediate proximity to the metropolis by "daily bread" trains. The house would be desecrated by being called a villa; still it must be classed amongst residences of the *rus in urbe* description, but of the good old-fashioned sort, inasmuch as it is a century or more old, and of a handsome red-brick elevation. The pleasure grounds are ample, with enough pasture land to support a fancy herd of cows, but with not enough of elbow-room for the varied out-of-door occupations of a country gentleman.

Inside the house, at the time of which we speak, were evidences of wealth and taste. Statuary, paintings, ornamental china, and objects of art adorned the rooms, perhaps somewhat heterogeneous of their kind, but all worthy of inspection. Nor were there wanting on the walls portraits, not of family ancestors, but of old and intimate friends of the proprietor, sketch likenesses valued by him less as works of art than for their individuality, reminding him of early friendships. Outside the walls everything was in apple-pie order. The broad, cheerful terrace overlooking the river, the exquisite lawn, the smooth gravel paths and neatly trimmed borders, the choice shrubs carefully disposed with ample room to spread, the plot of pasture land well farmed, the buildings and fences in perfect condition—all betokened, not only wealth and taste, but the prodigal employment of labour under the personal supervision of the owner.

In this house lived and died the Earl of

Drayton. He had entered his tenth decade
at the time of his death. His was no ordinary
character, and his had been no ordinary
career. He had commenced his long life in
the Guards, and was with Sir John Moore's
army in the advance from Salamanca to
attack Soult, and in the subsequent disastrous
retreat to Corunna. He was often urged by
his few intimate friends to commit to writing
some record of his long life; and few had
more power with his pen than he. Such a
memoir would undoubtedly have been full of
both public and private interest, for not only
had he lived in stirring times, but had seen
as much of travel, sport, and adventure, as
much of life in its various phases, good and
evil, as any man of his generation. But to a
handsome person, fascinating manners, appreci-
ative nature, ready wit, and retentive memory,
were united, to say the truth, strong passions
and a determined will. These defects in his
character had drawn him into errors which
society does not easily forgive. His earlier

experiences were unquestionably tinged with
bitterness and regret, and he was wont to
remark that his past life had better be forgotten.
This led to his shunning society and seeking
occupation in his own special pursuits. No
man was better acquainted with everything
relating to manual labour. A model of
physical strength himself, he could handle a
pick or a spade as well as the strongest of
his labourers; and late in life, when his bodily
energies failed him, he would still be in the
open air all day long, wet or dry, directing
and superintending his out-of-door occupations. To the men whom he thus employed
he was a liberal and open-handed master, but
his generosity was not restricted to those who
served him; all, of every grade, who were
brought in contact with him acknowledged
that he was a noble giver. Like Wolsey, "in
bestowing he was most princely."

Many traits might be given of the earl's
strong will and generous but eccentric character, and yet a volume would remain un-

written for want of his own graphic pen or
a Boswell to fill it. At no time was he so
pertinacious and energetic as in the purchase
of any residence which took his fancy. His
spacious old family seat in Shropshire, with
its beautifully timbered park, strange to say,
possessed no attractions for him. He had not
lived there for more than fifty years, not since
his marriage. He delighted in the neighbourhood of the Thames. The river provided him
readily with the exercise and amusement
which he loved. He was out every day on
the water in his four-oared boat, himself, his
valet, and two regularly retained watermen
forming the crew. When he was at his best
he performed for a wager a feat which has
never since been equalled, and that was rowing
from Oxford to Westminster Bridge in fourteen
hours. There were no outriggers in those
days; his boat was an ordinary tub four-oar,
and he rowed stroke in it. The course was
cleared throughout, the locks being all opened
and ready for him, the lock-keepers having

had notice of the wager. His pluck carried
him through to the end, and he won the
wager; but on arriving at Westminster Bridge
he was taken out of the boat senseless, and
on recovering consciousness found himself the
following morning in bed at a friend's house
in St. James' Street.

He purchased and possessed at various
times no less than six places on or in the
immediate neighbourhood of the Thames.
Each place, as he bought it, he altered, added
to, and adorned, buying up adjacent bits and
awkward corners with a determination which
the owners could seldom resist, completing
the ring fence, planting and improving, often
working with his own hands from the sheer
love of manual labour, and sparing no expense
in the pursuit of his hobby. When everything that could be done had been done in
the way of improvement, the excitement was
over, and he sighed for more worlds to conquer;
in other words, he sold the place he had
thus made and lived in, and looked about for

another to work upon in the same manner, and so on through the last forty or fifty years of his life.

In making these purchases he set all lawyers and legal forms at defiance. If he saw a place, and fancied it, he must have possession of it, if possible, on that very day. Never to be forgotten is the description given by Mr. Broderip, a most respectable solicitor of the old school, of the interview at his chambers in Lincoln's Inn between himself and his lordship on the occasion of the purchase by the latter of the first of these Thames residences. Whilst Mr. Broderip was one day sitting quietly writing in his room, a perfect stranger was ushered into him, announced as the Earl of Drayton.

" You have Aurelian House, sir, I believe, for sale," began the earl. " What do you want for it ? "

" Well," replied Mr. Broderip, " the price is £13,500 ; but—— "

" Quite satisfactory," was the prompt re-

joinder; "I'll give it. Pray, have you the
key of the house?"

"The key!" ejaculated Mr. Broderip, aghast
at the very idea of selling Aurelian House as
if it were a horse or other chattel—"the key!
Yes, I have the key; but we must have a
formal contract signed first, with proper conditions as to title, and an abstract of title
will have to be prepared and delivered to your
solicitor, and the title must then be properly
investigated by counsel on your behalf, and
a formal deed of conveyance executed by the
vendor before you can take possession. All
this will take time, and certainly cannot be
done before two months or six weeks at the
earliest."

"No," replied the earl, "that won't do.
I want possession to-day. Here's a cheque
on Messrs. Coutts for £13,500,"—(writing one
out)—"which I suppose is all you want. Take
the money and give me the key."

So contrary was this mode of dealing to his
usual practice, that poor Mr. Broderip scarcely

knew what to say. He felt, however, that he had no right to hesitate if he had the money in hard cash.

"Excuse me, my lord," he said, on taking the cheque, "but I don't know you. Pray let me send a clerk to Messrs. Coutts to see if the cheque will be honoured."

"By all means," replied the earl; "and I will, with your permission, remain here till your clerk returns."

The cheque was of course duly honoured, the clerk returned with the bank-notes, and the earl walked away that same afternoon with the key of Aurelian House in his pocket. The usual formalities relating to the title and the conveyance were all completed afterwards.

On the occasion of a subsequent and larger purchase the same summary process took place. The vendor of that property—a member of Parliament for one of our home counties—and the earl met at the chambers of the writer of these pages to negotiate the sale and purchase.

"I really cannot give immediate possession," replied the vendor, pleading against the strong pressure put on him by the earl. "My furniture, my library of books, my wardrobe are all in the house!"

"No difficulty whatever," was the reply. "Taylor's vans shall be at your door at ten o'clock to-morrow morning, and I'll be there myself, and help to pack and cart them all away."

"But," remonstrated the vendor, "I have twenty or thirty hens sitting in the poultry yard."

"Need not be disturbed," was the immediate rejoinder. "I'll take 'em all at a valuation as they sit."

Driven from one outpost to another, and tempted by the ready money, the vendor was at length compelled to yield, and the keys were handed over, as on the former purchase.

Yet again, on another occasion, immediate possession was as usual made a *sine quâ non*. But in this last instance the owner of the

freehold had not got possession to give. An
elderly lady was in possession under a lease,
which had three years yet to run. All
obstacles, it is said, vanish if they are reso-
lutely faced. The earl, having first agreed
with the freeholder, called on the lady, and
almost sent her into fits by telling her that
he wanted immediate possession of her house.

"Impossible," she replied. "I cannot go
till my lease expires three years hence. Look
at all my valuable china and ornaments," and
so forth. At last, dazzled by the offer of
handsome compensation, she was induced to
give some sort of consent, provided she could
get another house, not very far off, belonging to Lord Middlesex, to which she could
transfer herself and her valuables without
much trouble, little dreaming that the condition was feasible.

Off went the earl to Lord Middlesex, and
accosted him, without any circumlocution,
"I want your house, and I must have it."
It is scarcely necessary to add that he did

get the house, and returned to his friend the elderly lady in great glee, saying, "I have arranged it all. There's the house you asked for. Move into it, and give me possession of yours."

Returning by rail one day to the house which then belonged to him, on a branch of the South Western Railway, and whilst waiting for the train at one of the intermediate stations, he wandered outside the station, and stepping backward on to the trap-door of a neighbouring cellar, fell through the trap-door, which had negligently been left open, down into the cellar, breaking two of his ribs and otherwise severely injuring himself. He was then nearer eighty than seventy years of age. With his usual courage, he insisted on entering the train as it drew up to the station. But when the train arrived at the terminus of the branch line he declined to leave it, either feeling himself unequal to any exertion, or because he was satisfied with his quarters in the carriage. Accordingly the carriage was shunted on to a siding, and there it remained, with the earl in it, for more than a week, when the railway company, not caring that any part of their rolling stock should be used permanently for hospital purposes, required him to leave it, and he was then reluctantly conveyed home in a spring cart shrouded with laurels and evergreens.

Shortly afterwards the writer of these pages went down from London, anxious about the result of the accident, to see him. It was a hot, sultry day in August. The earl was up, half sitting, half reclining, in an easy chair in his library, with nothing whatever on him except a short white linen shirt.

> "His cutty sark
> In longitude was sorely scanty."

He had on neither shoes nor stockings, nothing whatever but the shirt. The gardener outside was sluicing the window-panes and gravel paths with water from the garden engine to moderate the temperature. Fastened to the back of the easy chair was a small

gibbet, from which was suspended a complete
skeleton by a chain attached to a brass hook
in the skull. In answer to an anxious inquiry,
the earl pulled up his solitary garment and
showed a black and blue bruise which covered
the whole of one side of his body, and which
any one else would have considered exceedingly formidable.

"That's nothing," he observed. "But look
here;" and with that he swung his arm
back and caught the rattling skeleton in the
middle, bringing it forward for demonstration.
"The doctor says I have broken this rib just
at this point, and the other rib a little higher
up nearer the spine—just here. I have got
this skeleton on purpose that I may know
exactly where the fractures are." He seemed
amused at his own originality, and certainly
made little of his injuries, recovering rapidly,
partly from his abstemious habits and partly
from a sheer determination not to succumb
to any bodily ailment.

Close to one of his riverside purchases there

was a scrap of waste land divided from his
domain by the turnpike road; the bit of
waste abutted on the river, and, wishing to
appropriate it as a convenient access to the
river, he proceeded to fence it in. The roughs
of the neighbourhood objected, and pulled
down the fence at night. He put it up again,
and again it was laid low, the work of repara-
tion and demolition being repeated several
times. At length he devised a plan of his
own to meet the case. He wrote at the top
of half a dozen separate sheets of foolscap
paper, "Lord Drayton proposes to give next
Christmas to the poor of the parish £200."
These sheets of paper he distributed about
the parish, one sheet at the public-house,
another at the butcher's, a third at the
chemist's, and so on at other places of resort.
He then proceeded to put up the fence again.
That night it was levelled as usual. The next
morning he went the round of the places
where the foolscap sheets had been lodged,
and made the following entry in each : "To

cost of putting up fence pulled down last
night £5, to be deducted from the above
£200." The roughs were amused, and the
next night showed their hilarity by uproarious
noises under his window. The following
morning another entry was made in the
sheets: " To noise and disturbance under my
windows, I charge the parish with £5, to be
also deducted from the above £200." The
rioters, finding their Christmas bounty likely
thus to dwindle away to nothing, mended
their ways, and allowed him eventually to
fence in the waste without further disturbance. At Christmas he distributed the whole
£200 without deduction.

Not always, however, was he successful in
his fixed determination to acquire any small
coveted corner near his house in order that
he might annex it to his domain. Twice was
he foiled in his object. Useless was his offer
to give each owner a better vineyard in
exchange, or to give more than double the
worth of it in money. But, though dis-

appointed, he did not, on either occasion, content himself by lying down on his bed and eating no bread. On the contrary, he was up and stirring, not sorry for the excitement of the opposition and for the opportunity for declaring war after his own fashion. On the first of the two occasions, the coveted cottage belonged to a laundress, who, as necessary to her trade, was in the habit of hanging out periodically her customers' linen to dry on lines suspended in her adjoining little drying-yard. The earl, nettled at her refusal of his liberal offer to purchase, proceeded to adopt strategic measures. He heaped up a huge pile of greenwood on his own field at an appropriate distance from the boundary fence, and, waiting for a favourable wind, set fire to the heap and kept up for many hours a conflagration, the dense smoke from which was blown direct on to the snow-white garments hung up by the poor washerwoman. All, however, was in vain. Like the historical miller of Sans Souci, the laundress held to her own,

and the earl's quick resentment ere long
evaporated with the smoke of his own bon-
fire.

On the second occasion the much-desired
triangle of land belonged to a charitable institution, the governors of which, men in the
first rank in society, were probably under the
impression that they could not or ought not
to sell any portion of the charity land. The
negotiation ended in a peremptory negative.
For the purposes of war the earl commanded
the position, inasmuch as his land was
bounded for the whole length by the road
which led up to the entrance-gates of the
handsome edifice belonging to the institution.
He might have fortified this position with
cannon, and as it flanked the entrance-gates
at a right angle, not a soul could have passed
in or out. He did not do so, but, instead,
erected an open marine-store shop in the
angle of his own land, the other angle being
formed by the entrance-gates, and in this
shop he exposed, nominally for sale, a mar-

vellous collection of worn-out iron pots and
pans, mangey brooms and brushes, old clothes,
patched breeches, old boots and shoes,
earthenware vessels of all kinds, some destined
to honour and some to dishonour, and mostly
of the latter kind, which were festooned from
corner to corner of the open shop. The
governors and their ladies (for the charity
was for female orphans, and much visited by
ladies) and all their friends were treated with a
full view of the contents of the shop and of the
garlanded earthenware every time they passed
and repassed through their gates. The earl
maintained that though he might not lawfully
employ cannon against his enemy, he had a
perfect right to keep a marine-store shop for
his own amusement. Of course retaliation of
this, or of any other kind, cannot be palliated
for a moment, but it should be added that
such tactics, if not purely and precisely the
"lambencies of spontaneous wit and fancy,"
were born more of humour than of malice, and
the evils were abated so soon as the immediate

8

effects of disappointment on his eager and impulsive spirit had passed off.

In the main his "lambencies of wit and fancy" were quite harmless in their origin. The writer of these pages had walked with him one afternoon to Doctors' Commons. Returning with him down Ludgate Hill the earl was pressed, for fear of fatigue, to take a cab. A vacant hansom was crawling up the hill, and was beckoned to, to turn round, the driver responding and pulling up at the kerbstone.

"No," said the earl, stopping, "I can't get into a hansom; I must have a four-wheeler."

Whereupon cabby, resenting the loss of his fare, shouted out sulkily, "If you didn't want me, why did you call me?"

"Don't you know, my friend," promptly replied the earl, "that many are called, but few chosen?"

At another time, coming up into the writer's room in Lincoln's Inn Fields, with merriment in his eye, he asked, "What's the fare from Waterloo to Lincoln's Inn?"

" A long shilling," was the reply.

" I thought so ; but the cabby who brought
me here wanted eighteenpence. I had only
a shilling in my pocket, which I gave him.
If I had found another sixpence I would have
given it him, but it so happened I had only
four penn'orth of coppers in my pocket, which
I offered him. The fellow still demanded
another sixpence. ' Well,' I said to him, ' I'm
going upstairs to my lawyer, and shall see
what he says to it.' ' Damn the lawyer,'
answers cabby, ' Give me the fourpence ; '
and pocketing the coppers, he drove off." A
finale which the earl retailed with great gusto
to his own lawyer.

After another of these professional visits
the writer accompanied the earl, then eighty-
five years of age, down the stairs to see him
safely into his cab. On descending the stairs
they were met by a cheery old gentleman,
little of stature, Mr. John Levien, who was
slowly ascending, hat in hand, mopping the
dew off his bald head with his pockethand-

kerchief. The writer, knowing that both his friends, strangers to each other, were proud of their ages, said to them as they met on the stairs, "Let me introduce a gentleman of eighty-five to a gentleman of eighty-two." "Eighty-two, sir!" echoed the earl, slightly lifting his hat to Mr. Levien; "I'll run you round the square for a fiver." Some days afterwards Mr. Levien called on the writer again, and remarked slowly and with much solemnity, "I've been thinking a great deal about that bet. I wish I had taken it." It is just as well for both the octogenarians that the race did not come off.

The earl's constant attendant during the last years of his life was an Irish maidservant named Maria, a little, short, square-built woman about four feet six high, possessing a bright face, even row of teeth, and a full Irish brogue. With her neat cotton gown, clean white apron, and sleeves tucked up above her elbows, she was night and day in attendance on him, doing the work of valet, chambermaid, and cook, all combined. The colloquies between the two, when the earl had grown infirm and kept much to his bed-room, were often most amusing, but they need the action, attitude, and brogue to be properly rendered. The writer had given the earl a dressing-gown made of rat's fur brought from India. He possessed everything that this world could offer, except, perhaps, a dressing-gown of rat's fur, and for that reason it was given to him. Though soft as the finest cashmere, he never used it. On being asked some time afterwards why he never used it, he turned to Maria,

"Maria, what have I told you about that dressing-gown? When did I say I should use it?"

"Plase, your honour, me lard says he's going to be buried in it."

One evening a young relative of the earl went down from London to his lordship's house on the river, intending to dine and sleep there. On arriving at the house he walked up to the earl's bedroom, expecting to find him there as usual, for being then ninety years of age, he seldom left it, except for an hour or two round the grounds in his wheel-chair. To the visitor's great surprise, neither the earl nor Maria were to be found anywhere in or about the house, and on further inquiry it was extracted from the other servants, who had been enjoined to secresy, that both had gone up together by train about an hour before to Hengler's Circus. The young relative instantly drove back to the station, returned by train to London, and proceeded straight to Hengler's Circus, fearing, from the earl's great age, that some accident might follow on this escapade. There, unseen by them, he spotted both the earl and Maria, seated next each other, in the front row adjoining the ring, enjoying the horses, and splitting their sides with laughter at the clown's jokes and antics. He waited till the end of the performance, saw them both get up and quit the building, followed them in a cab to Waterloo, took the same train back, and then a fast fly from the station to the house, and was waiting on the steps of the house ready to receive them on their arrival, as if nothing had happened, the earl chuckling over his frolic in happy ignorance of the pursuit.

He made it a custom now and then to give his labourers a treat to the theatre, generally to the Alhambra, always accompanying them himself and sitting with them side by side in the same seat through the performance. One evening they missed the last train home, whereupon he there and then set off with them on foot, though he was well advanced in years, and they all walked home together, some twelve or fourteen miles, not arriving at home till the small hours of the morning.

To these illustrations of strong will and eccentricity of character may be added his strange fancies in dress. At all times, whether in morning or evening dress, he studied the freedom which would have delighted our present reformers and advocates of rational costume—an open collar, showing a well-formed neck, enlivened rather than confined by a loose bright coloured tie, a vast expanse of white shirt, well suited to exhibit a magnificent chest, a short easy tunic, no braces, of course, nor gloves. At one time he took it into his head to wear neither socks nor stockings, asserting that they irritated the feet, and frequently in the evening at his own house he would come down to dinner in a blue coat with brass buttons and bright crimson trousers. Whatever his dress it always became him. A figure which, as a model, had been sculptured in marble from life and measurement by Macdonald of Rome, commanded admiration, however adorned, and never more so, perhaps, than when adorned the least. Free from vulgar vanity, he was conscious of the effect produced by his personal appearance, and was at great pains to preserve his figure to the last. He took regular exercise as a gymnast in his own bedroom. He was abstemious to a degree, for many years eating by weight, the scales being placed on the dining-table, and he seldom touched wine. This severe regimen answered in his case, and he could undoubtedly point to himself as the best evidence of its success when he inculcated its practice (as he often did) on some of his Sybarite friends.

A pleasant side to his character was his love of animals. A cat he possessed, which, from a bank overhanging a backwater of the Thames, would watch the turn of the tide, and, as the tide flowed up, bringing with it roach, dace, and other small fish, would dart down from the bank into the water, like an otter, seize a fish, sometimes even an eel, and carry it off for food. This cat taught one of its progeny to do the same. Monkeys and snakes were amongst his pets. A friend, on one occasion, sent him a snake from Sussex by post. On the envelope was written "Live Snake," to ensure respect being paid to it *in transitu*. Instead, however, of the snake he

received an official letter from the post-office
authorities in St. Martin's-le-Grand, referring
him, by chapter and verse, to the Act of
Parliament prohibiting the sending of certain
contraband articles by post, and amongst the
rest "snakes." In vain he wrote in reply that
this particular snake was harmless; in vain
was a long correspondence kept up as to the
genus of the snake and the folly of the pro-
hibition. No snake was delivered; the Act
was imperative. Many weeks afterwards a
youngster employed as a clerk in the head
office at St. Martin's-le-Grand, a *protegé* of the
earl, happened to call on him one Sunday
afternoon to pay a visit of ceremony.

"How do you like your employment?"
encouragingly inquired the earl. "How do
you amuse yourself?"

"Not much amusement, my lord," replied
the young man; "but just now we've got a
live snake in the cupboard in our room, and
it's quite a pet with all of us."

"My snake!" exclaimed the earl; and he

at once vigorously recommenced the correspondence, and succeeded in obtaining it.

The aviary in his grounds was a constant object of interest. He had wired in a considerable area of pleasure-ground, in which he left growing, in their natural state, shrubs, evergreens, and ivy, and had laid it out with gravel walks, connecting it with a building warmed in winter with artificial heat. This space was stocked with rare birds, many of which bred there, and the more delicate could find shelter and warmth in the contiguous building, flying in and out at will. The well-kept lawn was often as much enlivened by pigeons as the Piazza of St. Mark's in Venice. The garden tables were fitted with boxes containing Indian corn, peas, etc. As soon as he and his friends were seated in their chairs on the lawn, enjoying the summer's afternoon under the fragrant lime-trees, he would open the lid of one of these boxes, and the pigeons would come circling down in flights from their abode in the outbuildings, and light on

and around the tables, strutting and pecking
about in every attitude of beauty and ray of
colour.

These, it must be confessed, are trivial
traits and incidents, but, like specks of light
on the dark canvass of a Rembrandt, it is
hoped they may not be without their value.

On a graver subject—that of religion—it
might under all the circumstances be considered that, if anything could be said, it would
be better left unsaid. Perhaps so. But in
truth, no sketch, however hasty, of this
remarkable man would be complete unless it
touched upon his inconsistencies and presented all the opposite directions in which his
impulsive mind occasionally broke out. It is
certain that during the latter years of his life
he was, like old Lord Lyndhurst, in search
of a religious belief. In this pursuit he
scorned any assistance; he never attended
any place of worship, and was never tired of
inveighing against Church ceremonies and
stated forms of service. Still, he read, appa-

rently with earnestness, and constantly in his
sleepless hours at night, with the candle by
his bedside, certain books of devotion. One
book especially was his favourite, entitled
"Meditations on Death and Eternity," trans-
lated from the German by Frederica Rowan,
on the flyleaf of which he had written, "A
most excellent book; the more we meditate
on the sentiments contained in this book, the
better for us;" and whole passages of which
he had annotated and underscored with
characteristic force, according as they met
with his approval or the reverse. Firmly
refusing all guidance, and deaf to persuasion,
his reading, unfortunately, did not help him
out of the maze in which he was thus trying,
poor man, to feel his way, and resulted in the
simplest form of theism, namely, the belief in
a Supreme Ruler, and a vague idea of a future
state.

Returning to the incidents of his life, it
may naturally be inferred from what has been
already written that, consistently with his

nature, he was careless about money. He was in the habit of keeping large sums of available coin in a locked-up drawer of an *escritoire* in his library. To this he would resort when he had ready-money payments to make, such as wages and housekeeping bills, without troubling himself to keep any account of his expenditure. Free, and almost reckless, however, as he was in the way of expenditure, it did, in the course of time, strike him that the money in his drawer disappeared with extraordinary rapidity. At length, in this conviction, he was induced to mark a Bank of England note or two, so that, if robbery were indeed being practised, he might be able to trace the thief.

Suspicion fell on his butler, Houseman, who had been in his service five years, and who had previously been a private in one of the regiments of Household Cavalry. The police were called in, and the marked bank-notes were found on Houseman's person. There was no resisting this evidence. The

man was committed for trial, at the trial
pleaded guilty, and was sentenced to two
years' imprisonment with hard labour. Within
a few days after the sentence he voluntarily
caused to be returned to the earl from the
prison a sum of seventy pounds, which he said
was the sum total of his thefts, an act of
restitution which was duly appreciated.

Time passed on. The temporary excitement caused in the household by the event
soon subsided, and all was forgotten, when
after an interval which would about correspond with the term of imprisonment, the earl
received a letter from Messrs. Giltspur and
Bailey, a firm of solicitors whose business
was extensive, but partly connected with the
criminal law, desiring an interview with him.

The earl's habits led him to decline all
communication with strangers. Houseman
and the theft had entirely passed out of his
mind, and being at a loss to conjecture the
drift of the letter, or the object for which the
interview was desired, he sent the letter to

his own solicitor (the writer himself) to be dealt with as might be thought best.

The earl's solicitor thereupon called on Messrs. Giltspur and Bailey, who prefaced the conversation by requiring a pledge that the interview should be confidential, and that nothing which passed at it should be made use of in any way.

They then asked, "Do you remember a man named Houseman, formerly the Earl of Drayton's butler?"

The reply was, of course, in the affirmative, and that his subsequent fate was also known.

"Well," they continued, "the term of his imprisonment has expired, and he is now at large. He admits having appropriated, whilst in the earl's service, much more than the seventy pounds which he restored, and he is anxious now to make restitution of the whole. He fears, however, that by the present confession he may have to undergo another trial, and he has asked us therefore to intervene, and to require a pledge from you that no further proceedings will be taken against him."

The pledge, though already given, was at once confirmed, when the reason for requiring it was known, for none who understood the earl's nature could suppose for a moment that he would take advantage of a spontaneous confession of the kind.

" When will it be convenient for you to receive the money ? " continued the solicitors. " We have the money in our own hands ready to be paid over."

An early day was appointed, and the question was then for the first time asked, " How much money was stolen, and what is the sum about to be restored ? "

" Fourteen hundred pounds," was the astounding reply.

"Fourteen hundred pounds ! " echoed the earl's solicitor. " Is it possible ?—and this in addition to the seventy pounds ? The amount is so startling that no supposition can be too extravagant. Forgive the question,

9

therefore; has Houseman, after all, like Ananias, kept back any part of the price, or does he really restore all?"

"All," was the reply. "He does not know where to turn for a shirt to his back or a crust of bread to eat."

And, accordingly, the sum of £1400 was actually paid over in notes and gold at the appointed meeting between the solicitors.

The earl was moved to the quick when the interview was reported to him. He instantly sent Houseman £100 for his temporary relief, and simultaneously wrote to an old friend, the governor of one of our most prosperous colonies, with a statement of the facts, entreating him to interest himself in the man, and find some provision for him in the colony.

The appeal struck a sympathetic chord, and was responded to without delay. Houseman was sent out, free of expense, to the colony, and, at the instance of the governor, was at once taken into the employment of an influential firm of iron masters, who made him overseer and paymaster at their works.

Alas! about two years afterwards he caught a severe cold, which settled upon the lungs. Inflammation ensued, and the disease terminated fatally. He was thus cut off in the prime of life.

The sequel of the story, as it concerns poor Houseman, would not be told, nor would belief in the absolute transformation (some would say conversion) of the whole nature and character of the man amount to conviction, unless the following authentic letters were subjoined, one being a letter from Houseman to his mother in England, written just before his death, the other from the clergyman of the town where he lived, also to his mother, written just afterwards. Both letters are given verbatim.

" MY DEAR MOTHER,

" Once again ' mail day ' has come round, and I am glad to write a few lines, which I hope will find you ever comforted, more and more, to bear the burden and heat of the day by the strength which the Lord gives plentifully to those who ask it; and 'tis ever a comfort to me to know that you, dearest mother, do seek and have, throughout your chequered life, sought and found peace and joy in the Lord Jesus Christ. My earnest prayer is that we may all grow more like our Blessed Example. Indeed, I feel full of thankfulness that we are spared through another year, and I trust that, though separated during the past year, we have been continually united by the Holy Spirit in prayer at the throne of grace. We must thank God continually for the friends He has raised up for us, especially for the exceeding great kindness of my late master. There seems to be nothing which my lord has left undone to help me in my new life, and, in helping me, also remembering you, my dear mother, without which help yours would have been a hard struggle. Those who do so much for the happiness of others are never forgotten by Him who knoweth all things. I must now tell you that Mr. Samuel returns home about the 25th. I hope he will be pleased with my humble efforts during his absence. Already he has sent me his thanks in advance, 'for the great interest you have taken in the business during my absence,' which he had heard from Mrs. Samuel and others. I am told that the governor also has expressed his satisfaction with my progress. You know, dear mother, I can see my dear old master's hand in all this. What would I give if I could recall the past years of my service with him; how much I might have done for him, who has so thoroughly forgiven me all! However, I will pray that, 'forgetting those things which are behind, I may be enabled to press forward towards the mark.' My ever increasing gratitude to my lord when next you see him."

The letter from the clergyman in the colony to Houseman's mother was as follows :—

" DEAR MADAM,

"You will no doubt ere this have
heard the melancholy report of your son's
death. I am sure his loss will be a heavy
bereavement to you. Let me therefore give
you a few details connected with his last
moments ; but before I do so, I must state
how generally he had endeared himself. He
joined our Church, and the regularity of his
attendance, as well as the reverential and
devotional manner with which he entered
into the services, soon attracted the notice
of the clergy. Having offered himself for
work in the Sunday School, or in any other
way, his assistance was at once thankfully
received and greatly appreciated. The Lord
blessed his efforts among the young men of
the Church. He not only exercised a wonderful influence over the young men of his
Bible-class, but also formed a meeting for
prayer. He was thus engaged in these labours
of love when he contracted the cold which
proved fatal to him. I visited him in his

lodgings (he had very nice and comfortable
quarters in a healthy part of the city), and
every care and attention was bestowed upon
him. But, in spite of all, he rapidly grew
weaker, and on Good Friday morning he
breathed his last, so gently and peacefully
that we could scarcely believe he had ceased
to live. About midnight he expressed a wish
to see me. When I arrived he pressed my
hand, and expressed his satisfaction at seeing
me near at hand. I spoke to him from time
to time about Jesus and the better land which
he was soon to reach, and endeavoured to
cheer his heart with the hope of the ineffable
joys of heaven. How happy he was! How
fervently he said ' Amen, amen ' at the end of
each prayer! Seldom had I seen so strong
and living a faith. About a couple of hours
before he died, and when he was very weak,
he said, ' Let us sing.' We then sang a verse
of the hymn, ' Just as I am,' and he joined
in singing tenor, as he generally did when
in health. There was something super-

natural, it seemed, in the tone of his voice, as if coming from the choirs above. I feel sure he then enjoyed a foretaste of the psalmody of heaven. His funeral was very large; in fact, if he had been a native of the place and a prominent public man, it could scarcely have been larger than it was. Although his sojourn among us was so brief, we can never forget him. He was the model of a Christian gentleman; his conversation was always refined and elevated, and if there was one thing more prominent than another in his life, it was his great anxiety to do good to others. His life, though short, has been full of noble deeds. His labours will follow him. He has left a good testimony behind him."

Thus ended a brief but interesting career. The earl died shortly afterwards at the last of the residences he had purchased and occu pied on the Thames. His end possessed a interest of its own, and perhaps a passir reference may here be pardonably made to it, because what occurred in his case, at the close, is in unison with the train of thought suggested by the foregoing correspondence.

As already stated, his life had not been pronounced blameless, according to the unwritten laws of society. His ruling passions, to all appearance, were dominant to the last, so openly—nay, so defiantly—that the rector of the parish, whose duty it was to perform the burial service, expressed the reluctance with which he undertook that office. Whilst the corpse was lying in the coffin ready for interment, the following most touching prayer, in the earl's handwriting, was accidentally found amongst his papers, evidently composed just before his death :—

"My God, my God, have pity on me and improve my feelings towards Thyself, for I have lost all power of prayer, though none of the inclination, and my conscience keeps upbraiding me with my neglect of prayer to Thee, and yet for the life of me I cannot

pray. Not that I have any feeling but the
very best and the very truest, and the most
sincere trust in Thy goodness, and hence the
cause of my terrible regret, for the very
attempt to breathe a prayer is as wanting in
power as if I was dumb.

"Oh, forgive me, and turn my heart and
let me pray, and not die like a dog, as I feel
I am doing, whilst I see and hear of others
supported by the refreshing comfort of being
able, as I am willing and pining, to raise my
voice to my God and Maker."

The prayer is given verbatim. It was
handed at once to the rector, who said he
could now commit earth to earth with some
faith in the meaning of the words which in
our Liturgy accompany the act.

"The web of our life is of a mingled yarn,
good and ill together ; our virtues would be
proud if our faults whipped them not ; and
our crimes would despair if they were not
cherished by our virtues."

FISHERY TROUBLES.

FISHERY TROUBLES.

THERE is nothing more remarkable in these modern days, with all their innovations and new departures, than the extent to which, notwithstanding the constant struggle to be off with the past, the past still holds its own in many of the common affairs of life. During the last forty years, quite within the memory of many lawyers still in active practice, we have witnessed, and are even now witnessing, marvellous changes in our judicial system, based on a strenuous effort to bring back our forms of procedure, which, like ill weeds, had been growing apace, to the domain of common sense. Within that period, John Doe and Richard Roe, impalpable creatures invented in the Middle Ages, but, strange to say, down to the first half of this nineteenth century, imported into every action by which one man claimed land held by another, have been swept off the face of the earth. Fines and recoveries, fictitious suits, which most absurdly were resorted to for giving effect to many of the ordinary transactions of life, have shared the same fate, and people now ask in wonder what they are, or how in these days we could ever have perpetuated such a strange piece of antiquity as a *Fine sur cognizance de droit come ceo*, etc. Imprisonment for debt has practically been abolished. Can it be believed that, within the same period, a man could have been arrested on a mere affidavit of debt, and there and then carried off to a sponging-house? The whole law of evidence has been revolutionized. Within the same period, no one who possessed any possible interest, however remote, in the result of a civil action was admissible as a witness. What pages upon pages have been written to define the exact limits of interest which would qualify or disqualify a witness! Now it is often made a matter of adverse comment if the parties to the action, the persons most interested, are not themselves put into the witness-box. And so we might continue through a long list of judicial reforms, were not the examples already given sufficient for the present purpose. Yet, singular as it may seem, legal antiquity still influences in a very appreciable degree the common affairs of life, and the acts of a monarch of this realm, who slept with his fathers upwards of seven hundred years ago, are still appealed to in order to define the rights of humble fishermen on a part of our coast.

At the time of the Norman Conquest, a certain large manor on the coast of Norfolk, the Manor of Snettisham, formed part of the archbishopric of Canterbury. Nothing was then too large nor anything too small to be swallowed by the ecclesiastical maw, and no distance from the centre of the see was held an objection to the addition of huge tracts of country to its estate. In this fashion, Stigand,

who, it may fairly be judged from what we
know of him, never troubled himself to inspect
or personally regulate his distant but valuable
Manor of Snettisham, had not much to say
for himself, nor probably cared much, when
William the Norman, wanting something
pleasant for his half-brother, the soldier-priest,
Odo of Bayeux, insisted on that archbishop
surrendering the manor to Odo. On William
the Conqueror's death, Odo rebelled against
his successor, Rufus, who accordingly ousted
Odo from this property, and granted it to his
own " pincerna," or chief butler, William
d'Aubigny. This William d'Aubigny's office
of pincerna seems to have been permanent,
for, on the death of Rufus, we find it still
held by D'Aubigny. And when, as then was
usual on a devolution of the crown, an inspection of the titles of the nobles to their
estates took place, D'Aubigny's grant from
William could not be found. Henry I., however, acknowledged it, and in 1101 granted to
this same butler a charter of confirmation, the

text of which is still extant in the muniment
room of the present owner of the manor.

It is composed in the curious dog-Latin of
the period, with a few Saxon words inter-
polated, running partly as follows :—

" Sciatis me redidisse et concessisse Wil-
helmo de Alboniaco, Pincerna meo, et heredibus
suis hereditarie, manerium de Snetesham cum
wrecca et cum omnibus pertinentibus suis et
portum cum applicatione navium, cum soctra
et sactra, et Tot et Theam Infangtheof, et
cum omnibus libertatibus et liberis consuetudinibus, in bosco et plano, in pratis et in
pascuis, in aquis et molendinis, in vivariis et
piscariis, infra et extra Burgum, et in omnibus
locis et in omnibus rebus, ita bene et in pace
libere et quiete, sicuti Rex Wilhelmus frater
meus dedit et concessit." This rendered into
English would be equivalent to, " Know ye
that I have regiven and granted to William de
Albini, my Butler, and his heirs hereditarily,
the Manor of Snettisham, with wreck of the sea
and all the appurtenances, and the port with

the regulation of ships with soc and sac and
Tot and Theam and Infangtheof, and with all
liberties and free usages in wood and in plain,
in meadows and in pastures, in waters and in
mills, in private fishing stews and open
fisheries, within borough and without, in all
places and in all things peaceably freely and
quietly, just as King William my brother gave
and granted."

Under this grant the manor remained in the
D'Aubigny family for about a century and a
half, when, on failure of male issue of
D'Aubigny, who had meantime acquired the
Earldom of Arundel, the estate passed to
Cicily, one of the daughters of the last
D'Aubigny, subject to dower of Isabell, his
widow, and by Cicily's marriage was transferred to her husband, Roger de Montalt.
His descendant, Hugh de Montalt, made a
settlement of it, whereby in case of his own
line failing, which happened, it should pass to
the Crown. Accordingly we find it in the
possession of Edward III. in 1372, for in that

year this monarch thought fit to grant the
manor, amongst a mass of other property, to
his son, John of Gaunt, Duke of Lancaster,
by which process the property became part of
the possessions of that duchy, and so would
have continued most probably to the present
time but that Queen Elizabeth, of blessed
memory, happened to die childless.

Speculation on what might have been, but
is not, has afforded matter for the pen of
innumerable writers, from Mr. Freeman, with
his "what the world might have been" if the
Battle of Bouvignes had not been fought or
had resulted differently, to the probable state
of England or Ireland if the Midlothian
speeches had not been made ; and speculation
on what would have happened in the Manor
of Snettisham, if it had remained Crown
property, would lead us high up into the
clouds. What really happened was this :—

The crown, on Elizabeth's death, devolved
on James VI. of Scotland, and, with the
crown, this manor. James was at Edin-

burgh. The news, pregnant with his fortunes, must be sent instantly to him. Happy the man who could reach him first, and great the probable recompense for his diligence. A certain Sir Henry Cary proved to be this happy man. "Bloody with spurring, fiery red with speed," Cary made his appearance at Holyrood on the fourth day after Elizabeth's death, thus accomplishing the transit in a space of time then little less than miraculous. Nor did he miss his recompense. The pedantic monarch cast about for something which, while really valuable, would cost him no pang to part with, and he proceeded to grant to Cary, by way of free gift, this same Manor of Snettisham in absolute inheritance.

The original of this grant also is still extant amongst the muniments of the present owner, and affords a very curious and amusing specimen of the convenient and flexible Latin of the period. It grants to Cary "omnes et singulas terras aqua maris antehac superinun-

datas quæ jam a mare lucrat et aridum solum
redact sunt et terràs aqua maris jam superinun-
dat quæ in posterum lucrat et aridum solum
redact fuerínt abuttan adjungen vel adja-
cen predicto manerio de Snetisham; nec
non omnia stagna, vivaria, piscaria, piscationes
wrecca maris, ancoragium, groundagium, jura
et cetera, quoque modo pertinent accident vel
appendent vel parcella ejusdem manerii," and
all this, "Tenendum de nostris heredibus et
successoribus ut de manerio nostro de East
Greenwich, in comitatu Kentiæ, in libero et
communi soccagio." This would, in English,
read, "All and singular lands by the water of
the sea heretofore overflowed, which have been
already recovered from the sea and formed into
dry soil and lands by the water of the sea now
overflowed which hereafter may be gained
from the sea and reduced to dry soil abutting,
adjoining, or adjacent to the same manor of
Snettisham. And also all pools, fishing stews,
fishings, wreck of the sea, anchorage, ground-
age, rights, and so forth, in any way pertain-

ing, occurring, or appendent to or part of the said manor. All to be holden of our heirs and successors as of the our manor of East Greenwich, in the county of Kent, in free and common soccage." The original deed of grant is sealed, not only with the great seal of England, but also with the seal of the Duchy of Lancaster, an addition which, on the occasion hereafter referred to, was found of considerable importance.

The verbosity of the grant which, at first sight even then, and to the modern law reformer inevitably, would appear astounding, also proved, on the same occasion, to involve a very important result. In the wind-up of the whole grant, King James declares that Sir Henry Cary is to hold all the privileges granted to him in as "full and ample and the same manner as any earl or duke or other person had heretofore held or exercised them." Try to imagine that in these words lay the key to the interpretation of a private right in the nineteenth century, and a complete answer to a hostile claim then made against a neighbour, by persons who probably had never even heard of D'Aubigny or John of Gaunt.

Sir Henry Cary did with his newly acquired estate much as might have been expected, namely, sold it within six months from the date of his grant. The purchaser was an ancestor of the present proprietor, then a Norfolk squire of fine old family, Le Strange of Hunstanton, who had held property in the immediate neighbourhood from the Conquest, and it has remained ever since with that family.

The Le Strange for the time being has always exercised his Crown rights on the fore-shore, taking wreck, royal fish, and so forth, and in consequence of the scarcity of small stone on the opposite shore of the Wash, in Lincolnshire, making a very appreciable revenue by sale of shingle from the beach. Until a very recent period no one disputed his title.

The larger part of the coast line in this

corner of Norfolk abuts inwards on low-lying
pasture land, famous for grazing purposes, but
liable to be overflowed by the sea in the event
of spring tides happening to coincide with a
gale of wind from the north. A case of this
kind happened in December, 1862, when a
single tide overran the sea banks and inun-
dated some hundreds of acres. In order to
check such calamities, and strengthen the
shore defences, Mr. Le Strange, at very great
expense, erected better and higher sea banks,
and drove numerous timber jetties, or groins,
into the beach, with a view to consolidate the
foreshore and accumulate shingle and stone at
the foot of the banks. In rough weather,
thousands of tons of shingle are in rapid
motion on this coast, and the timber barriers,
so arranged as to intercept the rush of this
shingle, gradually produce large banks of it,
which, in time, solidify and raise the general
level of the shore. At the same time, experience has shown that these barriers also tend
to attract large quantities of mussels and

molluscs, and these molluscs, in their turn, serve further to bind together and strengthen the banks and shore.

The temptation exposed by this accumulation of mussels, however, proved too much for the local shoremen, and they proceeded to avail themselves of it by means which they called fishing, but which was in truth fishing with rakes, carts and horses, and not with nets or bait, and to carry off and vend large quantities of the bivalves for their own profit. The result was, that not only was Mr. Le Strange, as proprietor of the Crown rights and fishings, deprived of a valuable property, but the foot of the sea bank and shore was weakened and depreciated, and the very aim and object of the creation of the jetties and barriers jeopardized.

Accordingly, Mr. Le Strange was compelled to take legal measures to defend himself and prevent depredations, and, as was natural, people were found to combine and dispute his rights. An action was tried at Norwich in 1866, before Lord Chief Justice

Erle, when the whole documentary title to
the manor from William d'Aubigny to the
present Mr. Le Strange, was produced in
Court, and overwhelming evidence was given
that practice and user had been consistent
with that title from time immemorial. A
learned counsel for the defence, unable to dis-
place the evidence in any way, and casting
about for something to say, objected that the
grant of James, being of property part of the
possessions of the Duchy of Lancaster, was insufficient, as being sealed with the great seal
only. The original document was put into
his hands, and his objection vanished. The
seal of the Duchy was found to be appended.
He then objected that the grant of James in
no way conveyed a several, *id est*, exclusive
fishery, because the words "several or free
fishery" did not there specifically appear.
"Let me look at the grant of Henry I.,"
said Lord Chief Justice Erle. It was placed
in his hands, "et cum liberis consuetudinibus
in aquis et in vivariis et piscariis." "That is

a free and several fishery," was his immediate rejoinder; and as James I. granted the manor to Cary to the same extent with the same incidents as any previous earl, duke, or other owner had enjoyed, the Lord Chief Justice held, as matter of law, that the present owner had the same several fishery as William d'Aubigny had.

The defence failed, and no subsequent attempt to improve it has succeeded, although, unfortunately for the owner's pocket, it has been more than once essayed. A second action was tried at Norwich in 1877, but with precisely the same result, and it is to be hoped that now, at all events, the matter will rest as it is.

Singular indeed it is, that the priestly lawyer who composed the phraseology of the monarch's deed of 1101, should in this manner reappear in modern dress in 1866 and 1877, to discriminate between the proprietorial rights of an individual and the general and promiscuous demands of a miscellaneous neighbourhood.

The TWEED, as most fishermen know, taking
its origin in a small spring on the confines of
Peebleshire, within half a mile of the counties
of Lanark and Dumfries, follows a course of
upwards of a hundred miles in length to the
North Sea. From its source to Carham the
river is entirely Scotch, from Carham down
to the western corner of Berwick it forms the
boundary line between England and Scotland,
and from thence to Tweedmouth it runs
entirely through English soil. In that portion
of the river which constitutes the boundary
line between England and Scotland, and which
is there a public tidal, navigable river, the
alveus, or bed, of which is vested in the Crown,
lies the scene of action of the following story,
a story which serves to illustrate in a remarkable manner the strong common-sense and
vigorous address of the late Master of the
Rolls (before whom the case was tried), which
put an end to a costly and protracted litigation. The result was eminently beneficial to
the litigants, although much the reverse to

learned jurists and antiquarians on both sides
of the Tweed, as they were thus prevented
from arriving at a decision on numerous most
curious and interesting points of international
and historical law.

Mr. Macbraire was the proprietor of the
salmon fishery in the Tweed, on the Scotch side
of the river, of which fishery he and his predecessors had had peaceable and uninterrupted
possession for a period far exceeding forty
years, and which brought him a rent of nearly
£400 a year. Mr. Mather was the owner of
the opposite fishery, on the English side of
the river, which was let at a rent of some £50
a year, the difference in value between the
two fisheries being accounted for by the fact
that the deep water was all on the north, or
Scotch, side of the river, and in consequence
the salmon always ascended on that side, while
the north bank was also more favourable for
drawing nets and general fishing purposes.
Some two hundred yards below this deep
water Mr. Macbraire had erected a " ford,"

i.e. watch tower, for observing the salmon as they ascended the river, the duty of the watchman at this "ford" being to telegraph the fact of the arrival of the fish to the men, who were in waiting at the deep water above, fully prepared with their nets and boats. The practice was for the fishermen to row their boats and shoot their nets from their own bank right to the opposite side of the river, as far as they chose, or found it necessary, and then to draw the nets across the whole bed of the river, but always landing them on their own bank.

Mr. Mather had no "ford" on the English side of the river, nor any suitable site for one of the ordinary kind, and so could not see the fish coming up, the result being that nearly all the fish were captured by Mr. Macbraire. However, in the year 1870, Mr. Mather erected a "ford" by anchoring boats on the north of the mid-channel of the river, and therefore in Scotland, for the purpose of watching for the salmon. Upon which Mr. Macbraire at once lodged a note of suspension and interdict against Mr. Mather in the Court of Session, in Scotland, and obtained an interdict prohibiting Mr. Mather from having any "ford" to the north of the mid-channel. So far for the first stage of the proceedings.

Mr. Mather, finding that he could not improve his own fishery in the way just mentioned, next sought to interfere with Mr. Macbraire's enjoyment of the opposite fishery, and soon adopted an ingenious *modus operandi.* It constantly happens that, during the winter, heavy floods and masses of ice, descending the river, disarrange the bed of the stream, plough out large cavities in the gravel at some places, and pile up high mounds in others. In January, 1872, the floods were unusually heavy, and the bed of the stream suffered greatly on the Scotch side. Mr. Macbraire, as was his invariable custom, proceeded to restore the bed of the river to its original state, by filling up the holes, and scraping down the accumulated mounds, these operations

being essential to enable the fishers to shoot
their nets without risk of their being destroyed
by the accidental unevenness of the bed. Mr.
Mather at once applied to the Court of Session
in Scotland for an interdict against Mr. Macbraire, in which he sought to have it declared
that Mr. Macbraire had no right to interfere
with the bed of the river on his own side. In
this, Mr. Mather was unsuccessful, so that
Mr. Macbraire, to commence the series, scored
two victories.

Determined, however, not to be beaten, Mr.
Mather then procured five enormous stones,
each upwards of a ton in weight, and sunk
them on the south, or English side, just within
the middle line, thus effectually preventing
Mr. Macbraire from drawing his nets beyond
the middle line of the river, and rendering
both fisheries practically worthless. Mr.
Mather could well afford to destroy his own
fishery at the *locus in quo*, because he
happened to be the owner of another fishery
on both sides of the river about a mile higher

up than the scene of contention, and the destruction of the Macbraire fishery resulted in Mr. Mather's catching at his upper fishery all the fish which would otherwise have been stopped by Mr. Macbraire.

This took place in the beginning of the year 1873, and Mr. Macbraire at once filed his Bill in the Court of Chancery in England for a mandatory injunction against Mr. Mather, to compel the removal of the stones. Mr. Macbraire proved by a number of witnesses that whether the river was entirely in Scotland, or formed the boundary line between England and Scotland, or was entirely in England, the invariable and universal custom of fishing was, that the proprietor, on either side, might sweep the whole bed of the river with his nets; indeed, were it not so, the fisheries, not only on the Tweed, but on every other salmon river in the kingdom, would be valueless. One of the most interesting bits of evidence given in the case was a report of Sir Robert Bowes, in the year 1551, contained in a book

11

entitled, " A Book of the State of the Frontiers
and Marches between England and Scotland,
written by Sir Robert Bowes, Knight, at the
request of the Lord Marquis of Dorset, the
Warden General," as follows :—" Att the last
convention also it was agreed betweene the
Commissioners of both the realmes that the
Scottes should have such fishinges in the river
Tweade as they rightfully had and vsed
betweene the boundes of Barwick and the
mouth of Ridenburne at the beginning of the
last warres betweene the said late Kinges of
England and Scotland. The vse of whiche
fishinge is straunge, for where there is a convenient landing-place for the nett vppon either
side, the fyshers draw theire nettes over the
whole river compassing soe that they always
land upon theire owne side. In whiche order,
as I understand, England hath more com-
moditie then Scotland, because theire be mo
apt landing-places vppon the south side of the
said river, then the north."

Mr. Mather's case was shortly this, that

Mr. Macbraire's claim was for a *profit à prendre;* and that no such claim could be lawfully founded on custom; that no prescription, or usage, could lawfully give rise to, or ripen into any such right as that claimed; that Mr. Macbraire's fishery was a Scotch inheritance, confined to Scotch water and Scotch soil; and that Mr. Mather's fishery was an English inheritance, affecting English water and English soil; and that no incorporeal or other right affecting English water or English soil; could lawfully arise by prescription or custom or otherwise in favour of Mr. Macbraire's fishery.

Here was a magnificent question for the learned lawyers of the two countries to dispute about, from court to court, to their own financial profit and the advancement of judicial and antiquarian learning. Unluckily for them, when the case came in the first instance before the late Master of the Rolls, he thus admonished the litigants : "If people like to indulge in their feelings, for the benefit

of the profession, I suppose that must be so.
I shall determine what I consider the strict
rights of the parties, and I dare say there will
be plenty of litigation after that. When they
have each spent three times the value of the
subject-matter in dispute, they will both be
satisfied. I have no doubt they will go up
two or three times to the House of Lords.
I have known a Scotch case of £20 go twice
to the House of Lords. They may fight for
ever, and the result will be that neither of
them will get any fish. I can see the sort of
competing rights they have, and unless they
come to some arrangement about it, they will
never get anything."

The speedy result of this characteristic outburst was, as is not unusual, a compromise.
The offending stones were ordered to be removed, but the right was given to Mr. Mather
of placing a "ford" for watching the salmon
just beyond the middle of the river, on the
Scotch side, the effect being to reverse the
decree made by the Court of Session in Scot-

land, and to make Mr. Mather's fishery nearly
of equal value with Mr. Macbraire's. It is
presumed that both parties were content with
what followed this arrangement, as nothing
more was heard about it.

AN UNEXPECTED REVERSE.

AN UNEXPECTED REVERSE.

MR. SAMUEL WARREN's novel of "Ten Thousand a Year" was written before the facts about to be detailed were known, otherwise he might have been accused of plagiarism in constructing his admirable story on materials which were previously in existence, and on a plot which had already been developed. But Reality and Fiction tread upon each other's heels in a perpetual circle. Whenever some imaginative novelist or dramatist has taxed his invention to the utmost, Reality steps in and claims the story as its own, be it ever so sensational.

Sir William Severn, an English gentleman of good family and position, some years ago married the only child and heiress of Mr. Callaghan, who had for forty years or more

carried on an extensive and lucrative practice
as a solicitor in Dublin. On the death of
his father-in-law, Sir William Severn became
possessed, in right of his wife, of considerable
landed estates in the south of Ireland, the
rental of which, when he took possession,
could not have been far short of £10,000 a
year.

Mr. Callaghan had enjoyed these estates
uninterruptedly for fifteen years as owner.
They had been left to him, as will be afterwards seen, by the will of Henry, late Earl of
Monkstown, absolutely, but encumbered with
debt. The predecessors of the earl had
lived in the last days of Irish prodigality.
The Irish landowner of former days, as described by one of his own countrymen, Charles
Lever, than whom none better understood
the national character, contrived to have a
confused way of managing his exchequer.
No tenant on his property precisely knew
what he owed for rent, and, as no record was
kept of what he paid, the income was ob-

tained rather after the manner of levying a
tribute than receiving a legal debt. Meanwhile the proprietor pushed his credit like a
new colony. Whenever a loan was to be
obtained he thought nothing of ten or twelve
per cent., and, as he kept a merry house, a
good cook, good claret, and had the best pack
of beagles in the country, the creditor must
have been a hard man who pushed matters to
extremities. But there is necessarily a limit
to everything. Debts, mortgages, judgments
accumulated. Litigation followed. The simple
method of shooting the plaintiff, or even the
sub-sheriff, would not clear off old scores, and
so, after a long struggle with pride and poverty,
the proprietor ultimately had to clear out and
leave his estate to be ground into costs.

The estates in question, though heavily
burdened, had not quite reached that climax
when Mr. Callaghan undertook the management of them as agent for the successive
Earls of Monkstown. He was a man of great
courage and ability. On accepting the agency

he set to work to get rid of complications, to investigate and arrange the debts, to look into the accounts, to collect arrears, and place the tenancies and rents on a proper working footing; in short, he acted for and accounted to his employers for a period of twenty years or so as a competent agent should do.

After he became owner, he threw himself into his duties, as proprietor, with the same energy, but of course with more independence and liberty. Those were the worst of times for unhappy Ireland—worse, if possible, than the present. Callaghan did his utmost to mitigate the dreadful distress occasioned by cholera and the potato famine. He made many judicious improvements, abolished the middleman system by consolidating small holdings as they fell out of lease. He erected good buildings, and encouraged the tenantry to do the same, and carried out drainage and other works on an extensive scale. After his death, his son-in-law, Sir William Severn, followed in his footsteps so effectually and with such kindly feeling, that the tenants proclaimed him, though English by birth, to be an Irishman of the genuine stamp. The successive ownerships of Mr. Callaghan and Sir William Severn and all these acts and duties extended over a period of nineteen years. One year more, and the title could never have been impeached. Twenty years' possession would have barred any adverse claim, and conferred an indefeasible title on the owner against the world.

In the twentieth year, however, Sir William Severn's ownership, strongly fortified as it was by such a long possession, was attacked, and a litigation was launched, the gravity of which could scarcely be exaggerated.

Now we revert to the circumstances under which Mr. Callaghan became possessed of the estates. Henry, late Earl of Monkstown, the former owner of the estates, had inherited them with the earldom. With the estates he inherited also the encumbrances with which they had been burdened by his predecessor.

The earl had entered life with many advantages. As a young man, before his accession to the title, he had a seat in the House of Commons. He was well read, was endowed with great natural gifts, of shrewd intellect, attractive manners, and unusual powers of conversation. But as he advanced in life a great change came over him. He contracted habits of recklessness and intemperance, which by degrees led him to shun all society. He fell into a state of indifference as to his social position and social duties. Possibly the load of his embarrassments may have forced him to seek for solace in an indulgence to which many wise and noble natures have yielded before him. He left England, dropped his title, and assumed a feigned name. He never married, but whilst residing in the south of France he made the acquaintance of a French lady, the wife or widow of an apothecary at Bordeaux, and she consented to reside with him and to take care of his house. With her he afterwards returned to England, and they lived in retirement together for a few years, he retaining his assumed name and calling her his sister. Her health subsequently necessitated a warmer climate, and they went together on her account to Lisbon, where they resided all one winter, and where she died.

The earl then returned to England alone and disconsolate. On arriving in London he put up at an hotel in Piccadilly, which he had been accustomed to frequent when in England. Shortly after his arrival he strolled out one night to see the great fire at the Tower of London, which occurred at that time. He caught a violent cold from exposure, and it proved to be his last illness. He was ill about three weeks in the hotel, and there he died at the age of forty-five.

All these years, it will be remembered,— that is, since the accession of the earl and for many years previously—Mr. Callaghan, in Dublin, had been the agent and manager of the estates. Absenteeism, that blot on the

escutcheon of Irish landlords, had invested
Callaghan with the character of landlord. He
received the rents, kept down the interest
of the encumbrances, satisfied the pressing
demands of creditors, and controlled the expenditure. Though the accounts were regularly submitted to and ostensibly audited by
the earl, his self-indulgent habits made the
task repugnant to him. He cared for little
so long as he was supplied with money when
he wanted it. The money was found by
Callaghan as it was required, and the earl
was content. The result was that Mr. Callaghan, who, as a legitimate act of good
management, had paid off the old debts on
the estates out of his own money, thus constituting himself the principal creditor, and
who had since taken security for his fresh
advances, was not only the *de facto* landlord,
but had a very large hold over the estates
for the total sum due to him. The earl, by
his eccentric and intemperate habits, had
estranged himself from all his relations.

They, in their turn, were ashamed of him and had abandoned him. He had no one to whom to turn for help or advice. His only friends, the only persons with whom he had consorted for years, or kept up any sort of intercourse, were the French lady—his so-called sister—who had lived with him and had lately passed away at Lisbon, and Mr. Callaghan, his solicitor and agent in Dublin.

Such was the state of affairs when the earl was seized with mortal illness and was lying friendless and alone at the hotel in London. In former days he had been introduced by his French companion to Mr. Peach, a London solicitor, who had acted for her in some small matters of English business. Mr. Peach was known, as it happened, to the landlady of the hotel, and was sent for by her as the only friend she could think of in such an emergency. Peach came, and seeing the alarming condition of the earl, he at once wrote to Mr. Callaghan in Dublin, begging him to come to London. Mr. Callaghan lost no time in

obeying the summons, and arrived in London
with all speed.

With the events which occurred in and
about the bedchamber of the dying man three
persons only were acquainted. The earl himself was one; he was dead. Mr. Callaghan
was another; he was dead. Mr. Peach was
the third; he, when the proceedings were
instituted, was the only survivor, and by him
alone could the facts be narrated. He stated
—with what truth, who can say?—that, on
Mr. Callaghan's arrival at the hotel, they had
some conversation between themselves as to
the necessity for Lord Monkstown to make
a will. The next day Peach called at the
hotel, and found the earl very ill and in great
pain. It was some time before he could get
him to speak on the subject of his will.
Some conversation, however, eventually took
place, which the earl began by saying, "I
have no business to make a will without I
like." On which Mr. Peach remarked, "Of
course it rests with yourself. But have you

considered what would become of your property should you die without a will?" The earl then made some observation to the effect that it would be but fair towards Callaghan to leave a will to protect him from the creditors, or that he wished to leave him his property as he had already a great stake in his affairs. The instructions were accordingly taken down in writing by Peach at the earl's dictation, and, on coming to a proposal to give an annuity of £100 to the son of the French lady, Peach remarked that it would be but a small income. The earl replied that he had made a separate provision for the young man, and that *the estates would not bear more.* Subject to the payment of that annuity, Lord Monkstown bequeathed all his freehold and personal estate to Mr. Callaghan, and appointed him residuary legatee and executor. From these instructions the draft of a will was prepared by Mr. Peach and submitted to Mr. Callaghan, who, on being told what Lord Monkstown had said about

the annuity, smiled and said, "Just so; that
shows that the earl knows more about his
affairs than his friends give him credit for."
Some trifling additions having been made to
the draft by Callaghan, the will was engrossed,
and was executed the following day by the
earl, in the presence of Mr. Peach and his
managing clerk.

Lord Monkstown died about a fortnight
after making this will. His funeral was
attended by several of his relations. The
will was read after the funeral, and, as the
alienation of the property from the family
occasioned much surprise, inquiries were set
on foot by those most concerned in impugning
the will as to the mental capacity of the earl
and his free power of disposition.

Now comes another London solicitor on the
scene. Mr. Callaghan being about to return
to Dublin, referred these inquiries to Mr.
Westwood as being on the spot in London.

Who was Mr. Westwood? He was at that
time a partner in a respectable firm of solicitors

practising in London. He had been employed
for many years prior to the earl's accession,
and subsequently, in certain trust arrangements for realizing the family estates both in
England and Ireland for the benefit of the
creditors. Under this trust the English
estates had been sold, and a large amount of
encumbrances paid off. Westwood had acted
as the solicitor for the trustees in the sale of
the English estates, and also in an attempted
sale by auction during the earl's life of the
Irish estates. This latter sale, however, had
proved abortive for want of bidders, and the
Irish estates remained unsold.

Mr. Westwood was thus conversant with all
the circumstances, and able from his own
knowledge to afford all the information that
could be required. Mr. Callaghan therefore
referred the inquirers to him. Besides satisfying the inquiries as to the earl's mental
capacity and free power of disposition, Mr.
Westwood was able to explain, and did explain, that the Irish estates were so heavily

encumbered .as to be of little or no value.
And to impart this information more publicly,
Westwood framed with his own hand, and
caused to be inserted in the Irish newspapers,
the following paragraph :—

" We understand from undoubted authority
that the statement respecting the estates of
the late Earl of Monkstown, which appeared
in the columns of some of our contemporaries
last week, was erroneous, the real facts being
that the English estates of the family were
sold in the lifetime of the father of the late
earl to pay debts, but those proving inadequate
for the purpose, the Irish estates were deeply
mortgaged. The mortgages and other charges
affecting the Irish estates leave them so
heavily encumbered as to be of little value.
The statement above alluded to originated in
the *Limerick Gazette*, and led the reader to
believe that the bequest of his estates by the
late earl brought a vast accession of property
to our respected fellow-citizen, Mr. Callaghan.
We regret to hear that the mountain is little
better than a molehill."

Very explicit was this paragraph; nor was it far from the truth, for land in Ireland at that time was almost as unmarketable as it is now. A sale, it will be remembered, had been attempted, and had failed. The country was in an unusually disturbed state. It had been suffering from cholera, to which was afterwards superadded the potato famine. No time, not even the present, could be worse than the dire distress and misery of that particular period.

In that state Mr. Callaghan, upon the death of the earl, took possession of the estates as the residuary legatee under the will. Gradually, very gradually, an improvement set in, partly owing to a corresponding improvement in the general condition of the country, and partly to Callaghan's outlay and judicious management, in the manner already referred to, during his fifteen years of possession, namely, from the earl's death until his own.

During the earlier of these fifteen years many matters had to be arranged arising under the will, and in these, as in all English business, Mr. Westwood acted for Mr. Callaghan, professionally of course, charging Callaghan for all such business, including what he did in satisfying the inquiries as to the validity of the will, in the preparation and circulation of the newspaper paragraph before given, and in all subsequent matters.

Every year, as it passed, and every act thus performed, tended to confirm the dispositions of the will. But, unfortunately, during the same interval of time, the circumstances of Peach, the London solicitor who had prepared the will, were altering for the worse. He was gradually going down in the world. Becoming more and more involved, he had borrowed £1000 from Callaghan, which he was allowed to retain for some time; but being at length pressed for payment he became insolvent. By a strange coincidence of evil, something of the same kind happened with regard to Westwood, for on Mr. Callaghan's death, Sir William Severn found amongst his father-in-law's papers certain documents showing that Westwood had also in his keeping £1000 belonging to Mr. Callaghan for which he had never accounted.

Sir William Severn honestly, but disregarding the wiser policy expressed by the maxim, *quieta non movere*, required Westwood to repay this £1000, with a considerable arrear of interest. Westwood's partners were ignorant of the claim, and, when it was clearly brought home to their knowledge, recrimination followed between the partners, which led to a dissolution of their partnership, and to a new partnership being formed, excluding Westwood, who afterwards took new offices and commenced practice on his own account.

Whatever suspicions might attach to Mr. Callaghan's motives in placing these two men under pecuniary obligations to him, there is no doubt that the strict demand for repayment had the natural effect of converting them both into enemies, and dangerous enemies too— men who knew, or supposed they knew, a great deal, and were prepared to use what they knew in paying off the grudge they owed to their exacting creditor.

Acting in concert, these two men deemed it not inconsistent with all their past conduct, and with their loyalty to the will, at the eleventh hour, to impeach it. Both men have been long since dead. Let the credit or discredit of their motives and actions be buried with them. It is a fact, however, that they placed themselves in communication with the next heir, previously a stranger to both of them, and at their instance the next heir commenced judicial proceedings against Sir William Severn to set aside the will on the ground that there had been misrepresentation on the part of Callaghan, amounting to fraud, namely, that the will had been obtained by systematiclly concealing from the earl, whose mind was weakened by intemperance, the true value of the property he had to leave.

It may be easily conceived that such a case could not be determined without laying before the Court the whole history of the life of the late earl and the whole course of Callaghan's dealings with him.   It is not proposed to follow the case through all its voluminous details.   The outline already given will enable the reader to understand that it bristled with arguments.   He might, on the one hand, side with those who maintain that under no circumstances should a will made by a client in favour of his confidential solicitor and agent be allowed to stand; that family property, especially when connected with a title, should go in the direct line of descent; and that no lapse of time or acquiescence should bar the remedy against a wrong perpetrated by fraud. On the other hand, he might contend that the will had been prepared under independent advice, was the act of a competent man whose nearest relatives had forsaken him ; that his only friend was his confidential solicitor and agent, and being free to dispose of his property as he pleased, that none had a better claim to it than the friend who had stood by him through life ; also that there had been a long period of acquiescence, and that the party charged with the fraud had long since been dead.

Such was the ticklish issue presented to an Irish jury at the Cork Assizes.

The page is now open before us in which is inscribed that, for good or evil, the Irish are an excitable race, far more impressionable than the Anglo-Saxon. " One cannot dwell long amongst the Irish," says the popular novelist who has been before referred to, " without witnessing how generally poverty of condition and wealth of intellect go hand in hand together ; and as it is only over the bleak and barren surface of some fern-clad heath the wildfire flashes through the gloom of night, so it would seem the more brilliant firework of fancy would need a soil of poverty and privation to produce it."

With such a temperament it is not matter for surprise that a jury of Irishmen are unable to resist the sympathetic eloquence of their fellow-countrymen of the Irish bar. If the accounts are to be believed of the wonderful power of Lachaud, the great advocate at the French Bar, over his countrymen, the French must be equally susceptible. It is said of Lachaud that he could play upon a jury as on an instrument of twelve strings. When he raised his voice in defence of a prisoner the question was no longer whether the prisoner was guilty of murder, but whether the murdered man was not morally far more guilty than the man who had slain him. Englishmen, more phlegmatic, are seldom carried away in like manner, or to the same extent, by forensic eloquence. Nor has any advocate at the English Bar, at all events at the present time, the same power. We have many successful advocates at the English Bar, but none capable of appealing to the feelings of a jury like Lachaud in France, or Whiteside, Ball, Sullivan, and Brewster in Ireland.

The Yelverton case is a well-known instance of the power of the Irish advocate to move a

jury of his countrymen, and to carry them
away with him, and obtain their verdict on
every issue, except the plain one of facts.
The litigation in Ireland which followed upon
the short and simple will of the late Mr.
Colclough can be quoted as another example.
Having perfect right to dispose of his property
as he pleased, and having no children, Mr.
Colclough bequeathed his landed and other
property, which was situate in the county of
Wexford, to his wife. Who so worthy a
recipient as the wife, the partner of his joys
and sorrows, the true and loyal friend, the
patient nurse of his declining years? Yet the
will was disputed by Lord Rossborough, who
was the heir-at-law, on the ground of undue
influence. The question was tried before a
Wexford jury, who found a verdict in favour
of the heir-at-law, and against the widow,
partly, perhaps, because she had in the interim
married again. It is said that the eminent
counsel who appeared for the heir-at-law made
his most telling hit by holding up the will

itself by one corner of the paper between his finger and thumb, and appealing thus to the jury, "Tell me, gentlemen, would you disinherit the owld family on a rag of a pocket-handkerchief like this?" The widow could obtain no redress in Wexford, but the form of the proceedings enabled her to carry her case to the House of Lords, who expressed a decided opinion in her favour. They ordered a new trial before a Dublin jury, and she eventually succeeded.

So in the case of Lord Monkstown's will, the "owld family" was a strong element in favour of the heir, the next earl, though himself only a cousin of the deceased peer, and absolutely a stranger to him. On the other hand, the cause of the heir was damaged by the character of two of his most important witnesses, Peach and Westwood, with whom it was identified. It was possible that the jury would look on them as little better than common informers, for there prevails, even amongst the lowest classes, a kind of honour which revolts against such testimony, and suspects the cause which needs and is supported by it.

But "those who live in glass houses must not throw stones." We ourselves are by no means immaculate and free from prejudice here in England, where a jury are the arbiters. Occasionally even in our own courts we hear of an outburst of popular feeling. The judge, it is true, immediately interposes to rebuke it. "Silence," he promptly cries ; "remember, we are in a court of justice, not in a theatre." But the tribunal is inherently a popular one, and naturally influenced by what may be vulgarly called "clap-trap." Witness the recent sculptor's trial which has occupied the public time, at Westminster, for upwards of forty days. There we had the court crowded with connoisseurs and critics, a select and fashionable audience seated on the bench, the test bust modelled pending the trial and brought into court amidst the applause of partisans, the stage "property" in court re-

presented by statues of Byron and Hypatia,
and by innumerable busts of well-known
personages, from the Prince Imperial to the
Lord Mayor, or *vice versâ*, as the reader may
prefer—all combining to make an effective
scene intended to operate on the feelings of
the jury and captivating the senses of all those
who were present.

Dickens was beforehand with his travesty
when, in his celebrated trial scene in "Pick-
wick," he described Mrs. Bardell as led into
court supported by Mrs. Cluppins, and Master
Bardell being placed on the floor of the court,
in front of his mother, "a commanding position in which he could not fail to awaken the
full commiseration and sympathy of both
judge and jury."

Some attention was, in like manner,
bestowed on effect in the court-house at
Cork on the morning of the trial. Sir William
Severn (a strikingly handsome man) placed
himself on the barristers' bench, immediately
facing the judge, with his two young sons,

one on each seid of him—as much as to say,
" Have pity on us ; *we*, at all events, are innocent of any fraud or complicity." On the
long table of the court, under the eyes of the
jury, were spread out the voluminous mass
of accounts and vouchers which had been
periodically submitted to the earl in his lifetime, and audited and signed by him. All his
letters too—business letters and letters on
various subjects,—written to Mr. Callaghan
over a long period of years, were displayed in
bundles on the table—ocular proof that there
had been no concealment, and that the earl
was a man of intelligence, and capable from
first to last of transacting business. The other
side were equally alive to the necessity for
effect. The heir-at-law, an earl himself, presented himself in full view, surrounded by
influential relations, some of whom had held
high office in the service of the State, and
who had come over from England on purpose,
whilst the two incriminated witnesses, Peach
and Westwood, were relegated to the back

benches, to be well out of view of the jury,
notwithstanding that Westwood was acting as
one of the solicitors of the heir, and as such
ought to have occupied a prominent seat in
court.

Whilst the fame of the approaching trial
had spread far and wide, and had filled the
court-house to overflowing on the morning of
the trial; whilst the judge had taken his seat,
and all the counsel, solicitors, and witnesses
engaged for Sir William Severn had assembled
in court, what was it that detained the counsel
and solicitors on the other side? Neither
counsel nor solicitors made their appearance.
The court was ready and impatient—where
could they be? In the very nick of time it
transpired that they were waiting outside for
a pet juryman on whom they relied. The
train which was conveying him to Cork on
that morning had been delayed from some
cause, and had not yet arrived. This juryman
was a tenant of the heir-at-law, who had property of his own adjoining the disputed estates.

His name had been negligently allowed to
remain on the panel when the jury were
struck, and now he filled a very important
place in the proceedings.

On the arrival of the train all the counsel
and solicitors for the heir came trooping into
the court, looking as innocent and as uncon-
cerned as possible. However, the fact had
oozed out, and before the jury were sworn
the leading counsel for Sir William Severn
got up and prayed the court that if by
accident the name of any tenant either of
the heir-at-law or of Sir William's had been
allowed to remain on the panel, that man
might be ordered to stand aside. What a
vehement opposition was at once offered to
this appeal! Could any application be more
unconstitutional?   It could not be listened
to for a moment!   The panel was complete,
and the names of the jurors must be called
in the order of the panel!   However, the
judge suspected the little game, and at once
remarked that in a case of such importance

it was right there should be no semblance of partiality on one side or the other. The juryman, when called, was accordingly ordered to stand aside, and the twelve were made up without him.

The form of the pleadings conferred on Sir William Severn the right to begin. His case was accordingly opened by his leading counsel (since raised to the highest judicial post in Ireland) in one of the most lucid and effective speeches ever delivered in a court of justice. It can easily be imagined, without attempting to reproduce or even to epitomize the speech, that a skilful advocate would find abundant scope for eloquence in the materials before him. With regard to the charge of fraud, it would lie on the heir-at-law, he said, to prove it. Why was it not made and the question brought forward in the lifetime of Mr. Callaghan? The earl's habits of intemperance were admitted. Similar inconsistencies had been observed in many eminent men. " Ah," exclaimed the advocate, " who

would drag before the world the weakness of
the brain, the folly of the wise?" The heir-
at-law's claim to the estates was denounced
as the result of a conspiracy between two
ruined and unprincipled men, and every topic
was urged likely to operate on the feelings
of the jury.

The evidence followed, and consisted of the
voluminous accounts, vouchers, letters, and
documents before referred to, and of a string
of witnesses, including many expressly brought
over from Lisbon, all of whom testified to the
earl's general intelligence and capacity for
business, though some admitted to having
seen him occasionally intoxicated.

Then the counsel for the heir-at-law (also
since elevated to the highest judicial position)
addressed the jury. It can as easily be
imagined that an able and persuasive advocate
would have a good deal to say on the other
side, in addition to his trump card of the
"owld family." One clever stroke of advocacy
he had recourse to. Mr. Callaghan had pre-

served every document, every letter, and scrap of paper relating to this business. As the counsel sarcastically remarked, "Mr. Callaghan could not ask his friend to dinner without keeping a copy of his letter!" Callaghan always in writing to the late earl wrote a draft of his letter in the first instance, often on the flysheet of the letter to which he was replying, and kept the draft instead of a press or complete copy of the letter. All the correspondence was printed for better facility of reference at the trial, but the counsel, discarding the print, called for the drafts and original letters. These drafts he analyzed, pointed out to the jury the words originally employed by Callaghan in his letters to the earl, how certain words originally used had been erased, lest they might commit him, and others less significant in their meaning substituted, endeavouring to show by this means the working of Callaghan's inward thoughts towards the earl, and that they originated in a selfish object, but on more mature consideration had been cleverly concealed before coming into birth. The analysis had its effect on the jury.

However, on the [fifth day of the trial, and before counsel for the heir had finished his speech, one of the jurors was seized with illness. The doctor in attendance was examined in court, and pronounced it doubtful whether the juror would be able to attend during the remainder of the trial. As there were minors interested in the result, it was considered unsafe, after the example of the great Guillamore case, to proceed in the absence of one of the jurors, and the trial was adjourned.

Availing themselves of the opportunity afforded by the adjournment, the opposing counsel and solicitors met in conference out of court. Each had now to a great extent found out the strength of the other's case, and neither were confident of the victory. The whole of the subject-matter presented to the jury was dangerously inflammable. A fire

insurance office would have pronounced the
risk to be "Extra hazardous." Neither could
the tribunal be depended upon. Out of such
materials "the brilliant firework of fancy" in
the national character would have had full
scope in the jury box. The presiding judge
himself partook of the same temperament.
He was of an impulsive nature, and would
certainly, at the finish, have espoused one
side or the other with the zeal of a partisan.
His summing-up would, in reality, have been
a reply in favour of one side or the other.
Both sides feared the judge as well as the
jury. Under the influence of this doubt and
apprehension, the right and prudent policy
obviously was to "hedge." It was accordingly
arranged at the conference that the estates
should be given up to the heir-at-law on payment by him of £125,000 to Sir William
Severn, and that mutual release should be
executed and exchanged as to all past transactions. These terms were afterwards confirmed and carried out by an Act of Parliament.

When the result was made known in the county, the very same tenants, who before had proclaimed Sir William Severn as a model landlord and an Irishman of the genuine stamp, now displayed flags and wreaths of laurel, lit bonfires, and illuminated their windows in honour of the heir-at-law, the new proprietor.

DRY BONES.

DRY BONES.

As one who quietly steams down the river, bent on his whitebait dinner, and gliding by the *Dreadnought,* moored until lately off Greenwich, looks up at the wall-sided old ship and wonders how it ever could have walked the water at all, or have sailed or drifted otherwise than like a huge haystack, or why, when in action, it was not knocked into toothpicks, or burnt and sunk in five minutes,—so is, not the ancient mariner, but the ancient lawyer, who, sitting in the same armchair in Lincoln's Inn which he has perhaps occupied for the last forty years or more (and there are some still in that position), looks up at the pile of dusty papers stowed away on the top shelf of his room, containing the records of some old chancery suit, or at the top tier of

his tin boxes, labelled " Office Copies," or
" Bills and Answers," or " Charges and Dis-
charges," and lifts his hands in amazement
at that obsolete judicial structure, the suit,
and those stagnant forms, contrasting them
with the swift and simple procedure of the
present day.

And when he quits his armchair and walks
out of doors on his business, passing by those
old hulks, the buildings of the Six Clerks'
Office in Chancery Lane, and the Masters'
Office in Southampton Buildings, he regards
them with horror, for the remembrance of
what once, even in his own time, was carried
on within those walls, in the name of justice,
fills him with surprise that fire and brimstone
were not rained down direct from heaven to
destroy them.

Only think of the chancery suit of those
days as it involved the unfortunate suitor in
its deadly meshes ! It was commenced by
what was termed a " Bill." This was the name
given to the initiatory portion of the remedy

offered to the vendor or purchaser of a
property who could not or would not complete
his bargain, or to one partner against another
when the two fell out and quarrelled, or to
a legatee or beneficiary who fancied he had
been robbed, and wished to bring an executor
or trustee to an account, and was applicable
to many other somewhat similar cases.

The aggrieved party went post haste to his
solicitor under the delusion, wretched man!
that his wrongs were about to be summarily
avenged. The solicitor listened, interrogated,
collected and arranged the facts in writing,
and thereupon submitted them to his equity
draftsman (that is, the junior counsel, who
earned his bread by drawing equity pleadings),
by way of instructions to the counsel to
prepare the draft of the first formidable
parallel of the attack, called the bill. Now,
the bill was no simple statement to be treated
lightly and succinctly, as the suitor fondly
supposed. It was, in truth, an elaborate and
artfully contrived demonstration. In form it

was an address or petition to the Lord High Chancellor himself; and, in humbly complaining to that highest of all officials, the suitor approached him as "your orator," a dumb, injured, and perhaps impecunious mortal, but still "your orator" all through the bill. For instance, "Your orator humbly sheweth to your lordship that on such a day of such a year your orator agreed to purchase such a property," or "that your orator entered into partnership with the defendants so and so," or "that your orator wrote such letter or letters, or required and failed to obtain such and such accounts," setting forth his grievances in verbose paragraphs, every paragraph commencing with, "And your orator further sheweth that," etc.

Many of the statements put forward by a complainant in his bill were facts, some were fictions founded on fact, and others were pure and unmixed fictions devised by the ingenuity of the equity draftsman, who, driven to it by stress of circumstances, had perhaps advised what was termed a "fishing bill," that is, a bill framed by guesswork at the facts, in the hope of being able to fish out or extract, from the adversary, information or materials upon which to found a case which did not previously exist.

The facts being in this manner stated or invented in the first part of the bill, the next piece of the mechanism was called the " charging part " of the bill, wherein the defendants, whether innocent or not, in order to entitle the complainant in any event to some sort of equitable relief, were charged with colluding, combining, and conspiring together, sometimes fraudulently, and much more to the same effect, either directly or by implication, to the detriment of the complainant. To such shifts was the equity draftsman occasionally driven in order to frame in his bill a case capable of being equitably sustained, that the following *reductio ad absurdum* actually occurred not more than forty years ago before Lord Langdale, when

14

Master of the Rolls. An ingenious counsel only very recently deceased, arguing to support a hopelessly weak bill, was met by that eminent judge by the question, "Mr. Bates, if everything in your bill were proved, how can you make out any equity?" "Why, my lord," was the reply, "your lordship has overlooked the fact that this is a partnership case, and that I have charged in my bill that the defendant is a Quaker, which of itself is sufficient to *raise an equity* against him."

The coping stone being thus laid to the substantial portion of the bill, the whole of the previous portion of it was turned into interrogatories, every paragraph of statement being converted into a corresponding paragraph of question which the defendants were bound categorically to answer upon oath. Thus, " whether or not the defendants did on the day stated, or at some other time and when, agree to purchase such a property, or engage in such a partnership, or write such a letter, or decline to furnish such accounts," as the case might be, every interrogatory ending with "And if not, why not, or how otherwise?" These interrogatories, though part of the bill, were not considered worthy of the master hand of the equity draftsman himself. The stating part, or what may be termed the stomach, of the bill, when drawn, was handed over to his clerk, who mechanically converted each paragraph into a question, to be touched up afterwards by his master. The wind-up of the whole elaborate production was the prayer to the Lord High Chancellor, asking for relief, and which, like the postscript to a lady's letter, contained the pith of the complaint.

Now, what was done with this lengthy and complicated document when all was finished? Was it delivered to the parties from whom the redress was sought? Certainly not. That would have been too direct and sensible a mode of making known to the adversary the relief which was required of him. No; it was engrossed on long skins of parchment, about four feet by three, tied together at the left-hand corner, taken to the Six Clerks' Office in Chancery Lane, and there deposited or "filed," with a good fee paid on the filing. So soon as the defendants were apprised, by subpœna, of the fact of several sheepskins containing allegations against them having been deposited in Chancery Lane, their solicitor applied for, and in due time obtained, what was termed an "office copy" of the bill, namely, a dreadful scrawl on draft paper, the sheets stitched together at the top, issued from the Six Clerks' Office, and purporting to be an authorized copy of the parchment bill, but so illegible was the scrawl, and so inconvenient the stitching at the top, that the very first thing the solicitor did with the office copy was, not to read, but to send it to his law stationer to have a plain legible copy made from it for use, and when the legible and useful copy was thus made, the office copy was laid up in ordinary in one of his tin boxes, labelled "Office Copies," never again to see the light of day.

Provided with this copy from the office copy, the defendants either read it at the moment or not, as curiosity actuated them. Why hurry about answering it? Had they not two months allowed them for putting in an answer? The convenient season had not arrived. At the end of the two months they knew that they could obtain six weeks more time to answer, and at the end of the six weeks perhaps another month. Then, and not before, as the extended time for answering drew near its expiration, they applied themselves to the answer, which, in like manner when carefully and artistically drawn, was engrossed on long skins of parchment, and sworn to by them either at the Six Clerks' Office or before a master in Chancery in Southampton Buildings. If the defendants lived in the country, no officer out of London could be trusted to administer the oath. Though we have some five thousand or more such officers now in London, and distributed all over the country, none such then existed, and therefore a special commission was issued from the court to certain trusty and well-beloved persons in the country to take the answer. Of course the reader will say it was then sent up to London by post. There surely could be no suspicion of fraud or tampering with the answer, if, when sworn, it were sent by post direct by the commissioners to the Six Clerks' Office. Not a bit of it. The answer, bound round with tape and sealed up with wax, was handed to a special messenger, generally the guard of the mail coach, who, on payment of his fee, had to attend with it personally at the Six Clerks' Office, and swear that he there delivered it up to be filed in the same state as when he received it from the commissioners. When filed, a similar scrawl, purporting to be an "office copy" of it, was furnished to the complainant's solicitor.

Now, can it be believed that the net profits of these nearly illegible scrawls, called " office copies," formed the chief source of a very large revenue received by the gentlemen who tenanted the Six Clerks' Office? We are referring to the abuse, not to the men themselves, against whom nothing can be said. Each of these officers had his staff of writers, who scribbled off the copies at the rate of one penny per folio of ninety words, the suitor paying at the rate of tenpence per folio for every copy so taken, making the net profit ninepence per folio—a heavy tax on the suitor, payable, remember, not to the Government, or to the suitors' fee fund, but to private individuals, for which he received no benefit whatever. The annual amount of these net profits may be guessed when a mere reduction from tenpence to eightpence per folio in the charge for office copies saved the suitors in twopences alone, between March, 1844, and November, 1851, no less a sum than £40,886 11s. 8d. !

In the fulness of time it occurred to our law reformers that these net profits on " office copies " were an unjust burden on the long-suffering suitor, in addition to all the other fees he was required to pay throughout the suit to the suitors' fee fund; so they determined, instead of reducing the eightpence per folio to a still lower figure, to abolish the Six Clerks' Office altogether.

But then came the difficulty about vested rights and compensation. The recipients contended for a prescriptive right. The income in question, producing to each of them from five to seven thousand pounds a year, had been enjoyed by them, and by their fathers before them, for the office had the peculiar advantage of being hereditary. It was then the characteristic virtue of the British nation to respect vested rights to the veriest extreme, even in an abuse. At least, the nation acted on that principle when it voted twenty millions by way of compensation to the West Indians for the emancipation of their slaves. Ought not the same measure of justice to be meted out to the six clerks? The Legislature thought so, and, in abolishing the office, enacted that not less than three-fourths, *nor* (save the mark) *more than the whole*, of the average annual income of each recipient for the preceding seven years should be thenceforth paid to him by way of compensation, not only during the life of the fortunate victim of reform, but for seven years after his death ! Certainly, the nation could not be accused of parsimony when they applied the principle of compensation to posthumous profits on posthumous office copies !

The reader will pause and judge for himself whether, having regard to recent legislation, especially to those measures which affect land, the same extreme regard for vested interests and proprietary rights have been evinced by the Parliaments of the present day.

This digression will, it is hoped, be excused, for, after all, it accords with the dark atmosphere with which the Court of Chancery was then surrounded.

Returning to the bill and answer, it might

reasonably be presumed that, as each of the contending parties had now told his story, the cause had made decided progress towards a hearing. Vain hope! The answer, perhaps, disclosed too much, more than was anticipated, in which case the bill had to be amended, on the basis of a fresh departure, requiring fresh answers with fresh office copies, all over again. Or, perhaps it was insufficient, in which case exceptions were taken to it, and the cause was set down for hearing in its turn, not on the merits, but on the exceptions, and so on, through whole chapters of interlocutory proceedings, unintelligible to the general reader, pending which new interests may have come upon the scene, by reason of births, marriages, or deaths, necessitating supplemental bills and supplemental answers, in order to bring these new people before the court.

Well, the cause was heard at last, but only after a fashion. It almost always happened that the court was not informed on certain points of which it must have strict legal cognizance before a final decree could be pronounced. Order, Let it be referred to the master in rotation, to take an account between the parties, or to inquire and report on such and such matters, and reserve all further directions.

"All hope abandon, ye that enter here," should have been the sentence inscribed over the gateway of the Masters' Office in Southampton Buildings. Which of us ancient lawyers now living does not remember, and remember with horror, that sepulchral tenement, recalling also the drowsy divinities who presided over it? Roupell, Martin, Dowdeswell, Giffin Wilson, Wingfield, Henley, and some four or five others of their colleagues? Each of the masters had his suite of three rooms—the outer or clerk's room, entered by a door leading out of a long, dark, narrow corridor, which was the public thoroughfare; an inner room, in which sat the chief clerk; and the third room, which enshrined the master himself, whenever it was convenient for him to be present.

All business in the Masters' Office was conducted by appointments, which took the name of warrants, being printed forms, filled up by the outer clerk, handed to the solicitor having the conduct of the proceeding, and by him served on the other parties, who then attended the appointment accordingly, or, as often as not, failed to attend it. Thus, the first warrant would probably be one to consider the order. Then, at an interval of a fortnight or more, another warrant on leaving—we will suppose, for example, the charge against an accounting trustee or executor; then warrants at further long intervals, to proceed on the charge, and so on with the discharge—supported possibly, if the cause were a hostile one, by affidavits and counter-affidavits and documentary proofs, copies of these being, in all cases, supplied by the office to the opposing parties at the extreme cost to the suitor; only in this case the money was paid to the officials, not for their individual benefit, but on account of the suitors' fee fund.

These appointments were not few, but they were certainly far between, depending on the block of other business or on the convenience of the master; for he gave out his own days for work, and reserved what he pleased for holidays. The bugbear of a Parliamentary return of his official work being ever required from him stood not within the prospect of belief. And so the reference dragged on, two or three long vacations probably intervening, till it issued in the report, which was again the subject of protracted discussion, warrants to settle the report being innumerable.

The report being at length settled and signed, it was open to any of the parties to take exceptions to it; when the cause was again shunted on to a siding to be heard on the exceptions; and if it escaped being referred back to the master, as not unfrequently happened, it was set down to be heard in its turn on "further directions," when a final decree was pronounced, final only in the event of there being no rehearing or no appeal; and the suitors, if they did not always get the bare shell, were certainly not rewarded with the full oyster, for even the victorious combatant was heavily mulcted in costs.

As with the six clerks so with the masters. The voice of public opinion at length terminated the official existence of the denizens in Southampton Buildings, and in 1853 the masters were themselves abolished with, as usual, compensation in the form of their full salaries for the rest of their lives.

Dickens did good service to the public, when, in his "Bleak House," he called attention to the crying evils of "the system." Powerfully does he put into the mouth of the suitor, the man from Shropshire, a statement of his grievances. The passage is so apposite to what has been written in the foregoing pages, that it must be given in full; to attempt to abridge it would weaken the force of the language. "Mr. Jarndyce," the suitor said, "consider my case. As true as there is a heaven above us, this is my case. I am one of two brothers. My father (a farmer) made a will, and left his farm and stock and so forth to my mother for her life. After my mother's death, all was to come to me, except a legacy of three hundred pounds that I was then to pay to my brother. My mother died. My brother some time afterwards claimed his legacy. I, and some of my relations, said that he had had a part of it already, in board and lodging and some other things. Now mind! That was the question, and nothing else. No one disputed the will; no one disputed anything, but whether part of that three hundred pounds had been already paid or not. To settle that question, my brother, filing a bill, I was obliged to go into this accursed Chancery; I was forced there because the law forced me, and would let me go nowhere else. Seventeen people were made defendants to that simple suit! It first came on after two years. It was then stopped for another two years, while the master (may his head rot off!) inquired whether I was my father's son —about which there was no dispute at all with any mortal creature. He then found out that there were not defendants enough—remember, there were only seventeen as yet !— but we must have another who had been left out, and must begin all over again. The costs at that time—before the thing was begun !— were three times the legacy. My brother would have given up the legacy, and joyful to escape more costs. My whole estate left to me, in that will of my father's, has gone in costs. The suit, still undecided, has fallen into rack and ruin and despair, with everything else—and here I stand this day !'' And in another part of the book, the indignant but tenderhearted and sympathetic author, speaking in his own name, denounces " the system " in language as true as it strong, " This is the Court of Chancery, which has its decaying houses and its blighted lands in every shire, which has its ruined suitors, which gives to

monied might the means of abundantly
wearying out the right, which so exhausts
finances, patience, courage, hope, so over-
throws the brain and breaks the heart, that
there is not an honourable man among its
practitioners who would not give—who does
not often give—the warning, ' Suffer any
wrong that can be done you, rather than come
here ! ' "

Such are the recollections of a race of
lawyers now rapidly diminishing in number.
The new generation have happily been spared
the labour, as well as the shame, of acquiring
the arts and tactics, the tricks and devices,
involved in such a practice, and can address
themselves in the present day to honest
means of ascertaining the truth which ought
to be the sole object of every judicial system.
If both parties to any litigation are now really
desirous that a fair and proper decision of the
matters in dispute should be attained, the
system will assist, instead of retarding, that
result; whilst, however, it must be added that,

15

so long as human nature remains unchanged, no improvement of procedure nor amendment of form can or ever will prevent delay and obstruction where one of the litigants is dishonestly determined to withstand the course of law.

THE CARRON COMPANY.

THE CARRON COMPANY.

ALL the actors in the following drama are dead, and have passed to their account. No question, therefore, affecting their personal position can now arise.

More than a hundred years ago, certain gentlemen at Sheffield, friends and relations of Scotch people of good position, took it into their heads to establish an iron foundry in Scotland, on the banks of the Carron Water, near Falkirk, and they succeeded in obtaining a charter under the union seal of Scotland, dated in June, 1771, constituting them a corporation with the power of holding land to any extent, and fixing their capital at £150,000 sterling, divided into six hundred shares of £250 each. Of the 600 shares 556 only were ever actually taken up and paid for.

The most active promoters of the venture at the time were a Sheffield man, Dr. Roebuck, a lineal ancestor of the late eminent politician of that name, and one Charles Gascoigne, of a then well-known Yorkshire family.

The company got into working order at once, commenced its operations by purchasing a site at Carron, and established Gascoigne as manager. The charter contained a peculiar clause, under which no partner was at liberty to sell his shares in open market, but was compelled first to offer them to the company itself at such price as he saw fit, and on their being declined by the company, then to the other shareholders at the same price, with no right to sell to a stranger until both the company and the other partners had formally declined, or at a lower price. Another clause of the partnership prevented any partner who did not hold at least ten shares from having any right of interference or control of the management. The modern system of boards of direction had not then come into vogue,

and every partner in this company who had
ten shares or upwards was, *ipso facto*, a
managing partner, and entitled to interfere
actively in the conduct of the affairs. There
was also a clause by which one per cent. per
annum of the annual profits was to be set
aside as a sinking fund, and the whole residue
of the profits was to be disposed of by general
meetings of the managing partners, to be held
annually in October; and there was, of course,
the usual string of conditions that proper
accounts were to be kept, disclosing the true
state of the company's affairs, and that such
accounts should be produced at the annual
general meetings.

The company for the first few years of its
existence did not turn out a success; and
Gascoigne, probably feeling his incapacity,
absconded to Russia with all the company's
cash he could lay his hands on. Many years
afterwards he returned *incognito* to Scotland;
but being traced by his creditors, he was
pursued to Tyningham Castle, and only

escaped by crossing the North Sea to Sweden
in an open fishing smack, which he seized on
the coast.

In the year 1786 the concern was at a very
low ebb, and the managing partners were
obliged to cast about for some competent
man of business who could take the management at the works, and revive the energy of
the company.

Accordingly, in that year they selected a
Cumberland man, who had originally been
a watchmaker at Keswick, but had a year or
two before gone to Carron in some very sub-
ordinate capacity, to act as resident manager.
The selection was well justified in one sense,
by results.

Joseph Stainton was a man of remarkable
ability and singular tenacity of purpose.
Under his management affairs were very
shortly brought into good order, and from
that time to the day of his death, in 1825,
he worked the company thoroughly well,
making it one of the most prosperous and

productive trading enterprises in the world.
Its business consisted of raising iron ore and
coal, and manufacturing crude iron, as well
as making articles out of the iron they themselves raised and smelted. A dividend of five
per cent. per annum was paid yearly from 1788
to 1805, when it was raised to nine per cent.,
at which rate it remained stationary till 1839.

It should have been stated above that, in
addition to the annual meetings prescribed to
be held in October, the charter directed that
there should be committees of managing
partners held whenever required to look into
the affairs, and such committees were, in fact,
held for some few years after the appointment
of Joseph Stainton as manager; but they soon
fell into desuetude in the same measure as
Joseph Stainton's influence grew, and the last
ever held, until the catastrophe about to be
related, took place in 1813.

Not only was Joseph Stainton a man of
first rate mental power, but he was also
possessed of the strongest family affection,

so far as that affection develops itself in a pecuniary direction. Not only did he himself enjoy the lucrative position of managing director, but he also gradually introduced into the company, to fill every office worth acceptance, his immediate relatives. In 1808 he made his brother Henry, a man equal, if not superior, to himself in ability, manager in London, a post which this brother retained till his death in 1851. A nephew, Thomas Crosthwaite, was appointed, in 1801, manager at Liverpool; and on Crosthwaite's death in 1830, Henry Dawson, another nephew, took his place. A third nephew, Thomas Dawson, became manager at Glasgow. A fourth nephew, Joseph Dawson, became sub-manager at the works at Carron, and afterwards, in 1825, on Joseph Stainton's death, chief-manager; and he in turn, on his death in 1850, was succeeded by yet another nephew, William Dawson; and other connections figured wherever wanted.

Henry Stainton (the brother of Joseph)

deserves a few lines to himself. He resided at Lewisham, near Blackheath, and was, it will be remembered, the manager in London. His peculiar hobbies were amateur hydraulics and the care of tame deer and wild fowl. He purchased for these pets a few acres of adjoining land supplied by a spring of water, and spent many years and large sums of money in converting these acres into a system of canals, reservoirs, cascades, and islands, at various levels by means of lifts and sluices of his own design. His habit was to rise at six o'clock, winter and summer alike, and to spend the first two hours of the day with his pets; the rest of the day he devoted to the iron trade. When not busied with his hydraulics or his pets, his whole thoughts turned on iron. Even Sunday was no day of rest for him. He was not accustomed to attend any place of worship, but spent the day on his islands ruminating on new patterns for grates and other castings. When the idea of a design struck him he would dot it down on paper, and send it on the following day to Carron. Society he never courted, or permitted to approach his house, either for his own sake or his children. Another curious feature in his character was the scrupulous fidelity with which he seems to have preserved every scrap of writing ever addressed to him, and the draft of every letter ever written by him. Nor is it unreasonable to infer that in this careful record he had in constant view the possibility (afterwards converted into actual fact) of there arising a necessity for the correspondence being useful at some time or other for his self-defence, or rather to show that he never sinned alone, should his partners and confederates turn round upon him to screen themselves. Notwithstanding that he lived at great cost, and made large settlements on his children, his personal estate was at his death sworn for probate at £400,000.

To return to the concern itself. The period under review may be divided into two parts, from 1801 to 1825, in which latter year Joseph

Stainton died, and from 1825 to 1850. During
the first period the profits of the concern were
very great, owing to the extensive business
done by the company with the Government
in the course of the Napoleonic wars, the
company, in fact, absorbing almost the entire
manufacture of cannon, and giving its name
(Carronades) to one description of gun.
Although the modest dividend of five, afterwards raised to nine, per cent. was paid during
this time, a much larger sum should have
been, but was not, distributed, because, it
would seem, the two brothers Stainton even
then had formed in their minds the design
which was at a later period carried out almost
to final victory, and which, but for internal
dissension, would have made this powerful
concern the sole appanage of the happy family.

Inasmuch as no partner could sell a share
without first offering it to his partners, it
occurred to the brothers that they had only
to keep down the ostensible value of the
property in order to induce their partners to

sell their shares at under value. At all events, and whether this design then existed or not, it is a fact that the published balance-sheets and accounts did not disclose to the proprietors vast accumulations of profits, to such an extent that the balance-sheet of June, 1824, being the last before Joseph Stainton's death, understated the property of the company by upwards of £310,000, no less than £109,000 of this large sum representing realized property, such as landed estates, canal shares, money lent, ships, etc.

After Joseph Stainton's death, however, in 1825, the scheme assumed a more distinct and decided aspect, and between 1825 and 1850 no less than £650,000 more was put out of sight, during which period the happy family so prospered in their scheme that they purchased up, either for themselves or for the company as a corporation, which virtually meant themselves, so many shares that in 1850, before the true facts came to light, no less than 328 shares, or more than half the

whole concern, were held by members of the
Stainton or Dawson family as individuals, and
154 shares (inclusive of the 44 never issued)
were held by the company, whilst only 118
shares were owned by independent shareholders.

The history of the boldness with which for
nearly half a century this family contrived to
suppress the results of the obstinate produc-
tiveness of the works is a most interesting
and startling record. The *modus operandi*
was twofold: first, by direct manipulation of
the accounts in the ledgers; and secondly, by
suppression and non-entry of assets. Each
half-year the managing partner at the works
was accustomed, for his own pleasure and for
the information of the London manager, to
make out a balance-sheet showing the real
profits; but this balance-sheet they cut down
and adjusted precisely as they thought proper,
partly by understating or omitting stocks in
hand, and partly by entering large sums as
debts due from the company which were in

fact due to it, a method by which, if the accumulations prior to 1824 were taken into account, something more than a million sterling was, up to the year 1850, quietly put by.

Having power under their charter to purchase land, whenever they saw an estate in the neighbourhood at all attractive in a mineral point of view the manager would purchase it, and would enter in the ledger to some new account the amount of the purchase money. The estate, of course, should thereafter have been treated as an asset of the company; but, as it would never have answered the purpose of the family to let their partners know the value of the company's property, they were in the habit of writing down these purchased estates year by year—sometimes very rapidly indeed—until after the lapse of a few years there was little or no record at all of such estates, and by this process the company became great landowners, especially of mineral and warehouse properties, without the knowledge of the non-official partners.

The most active period of this startling organization dates from 1830 to 1850, during which no person not being a member of the happy family was permitted to acquire a single share, the family possessing themselves of all which were offered at prices varying from £500 to £600 each share, such shares being worth at the time, if true accounts had been forthcoming, something like £2000 each.

Had the members of this happy family been true to each other, this gigantic transaction would never have come to light; but while the united family were working together to acquire all the shares of the company, Henry Stainton, the London manager, was carrying on an additional and private game of his own. Not content with buying shares whenever he could get them, he had accumulated in London an enormous private profit. His salary, fixed in 1825, was £2000 a year, with £250 extra for Government business; but, scorning such paltry remuneration, he had from the first chosen not to take any fixed

16

salary, but simply to charge the company what he liked for himself, and in his books to call such charges "porterage on wares," or "sundry expenses."

Up to the time of his death he had thus overcharged the company for his own benefit upwards of £200,000, besides holding in his own name another almost equally large sum of bank stock and other funds, part of the concealed treasure of the company. Feeling, as it would seem, his end near, Henry Stainton, in 1850, thought it prudent to recapitulate to the manager in Scotland the state of so much of the company's concealed reserves as he thought might be well that his partners should be able to require his executors to give up after his death, and accordingly he wrote to his nephew, William Dawson, in April, 1850, as follows :—

"DEAR NEPHEW,

"Not being prepared to do it from memory, I now make haste to communicate

the actual state of the *reserve* account, long
ago put in my hands for safe and secret
custody, being originally the outcome of the
Board's (*i.e.* the Board of Ordnance) account,
the regular produce to be added to the principal as my judgment might direct. It is as
follows on the first of this month :—

	£
Bank of England Stock, £30,000, worth say	60,000
Exchequer Bills, £24,000	24,000
Cash uninvested at my acting account in the Bank of England	12,046
Making together	£96,046

The whole, being the property of the Carron
Company, stands in my name, and it is
entirely unknown to any one here besides
myself. How far it may be prudent to communicate this fact is for you to judge; that
it should be communicated to the partners
generally would, in my opinion, be exceedingly
indiscreet. It was originally intended to form
a fund to meet any unforeseen occurrence in
the business,—such as, for instance, the present and prospective state of the iron trade,—

without making any *public* difference as to
the company's proceedings in money matters.
There was a further outcome of the Board's
account, as nearly as I can recollect, of about
£8000, which was carried at once to the company's credit—how entered in the Carron
books I know not, but this must have been
within the last twenty, or at most twenty-five,
years."

Henry Stainton dying suddenly in 1851,
and his own son and successor finding in the
books entries unintelligible to him, being the
before-mentioned "porterage on wares," and
the like, disclosed them to the other members
of the family, who soon discovered, or pretended to discover, the diversion of the
property of the company into Henry Stainton's
pocket, and, most injudiciously for themselves
as it now would appear, treated this son in
a sharp and oppressive manner, compelling
him to pay over to them for principal and
interest no less than £220,000 in one lump,

and a subsequent sum of about £50,000 on
further investigation, but with the result that
he (it is not necessary to say with what
motive) disclosed the whole thread of the
secret organization, from its conception to its
close, to some of those gentlemen who had
sold shares to his family at various dates
during the then last quarter of a century.

Those ex-shareholders upon this took legal
proceedings against the surviving members of
the family, with the detail of which this statement need not be encumbered; and after the
usual obstructions and delays afforded by our
then system of jurisprudence, those ex-shareholders or sellers recovered by compromise a
very large sum of money, exceeding £1000 per
share. Had the ex-shareholders been young
people ready to fight the battle to the end,
this £1000 per share return would probably
have grown into £2000; but they were old
quiet folks, only too glad to have their last
days made comfortable, and the result was
that the family retained by far the larger part

of their so-called reserves for their own · benefit.

Extracts from the correspondence of the members of the family with one another, which were discovered in the course of the litigation, illustrate in a most remarkable manner the courage with which the systematic accumulation and concealment of profits were carried out.

So early as the commencement of the year 1825, Mr. Tod and Mr. Romanes, two of the outside shareholders, not members of the happy family, were very urgent in their search for information as to the position of the company; and it is interesting to note how these men, who were men of business, were hoodwinked, and eventually wearied out of the concern. Here are samples of some of the letters written by the managers on the occasion :—

In April of that year, Joseph Dawson, the manager of the works at Carron, wrote to his uncle, Henry Stainton, the manager in London, "If the balance-sheet should be

granted, I think it would be advisable to state
the inventories in one sum, instead of stating
separately so much for the weight and value
of the goods and materials, and so much
as the value of the buildings and utensils.
According to the weight of the inventory of
the London warehouse, the goods will hardly
average £5 per ton. This might startle the
writers (that is, Messrs. Tod and Romanes) if
they begin to calculate."

Again, in May, " I enclose you a copy of
the balance-sheet, made out in the way in
which it used to be laid before the general
meeting, in which the columns are marked
which we now intend to leave out, and also
an abstract of the same, which it has been
customary to send to all the partners entitled to vote. I shall thank you to say
which we should send to Messrs. Tod and
Romanes."

Again, in October, "I am somewhat at a
loss how to write to Tod and Romanes about
the information they want, as it was promised

to them at the general meeting. I am afraid
we can hardly refuse them altogther, and it
would perhaps be as well to give them a few
general items at the meeting, from which
they could not obtain any real information of
any consequence."

Henry Stainton was equal to the occasion,
for in January, 1826, he wrote to his nephew
at Carron, "It is exceedingly necessary to
keep all real information from these gentlemen, to prevent them doing mischief; but in
doing so, it may be very necessary to keep
carefully in view that, in unavoidable intercourse with fools in this world, people
generally get better on by flattering than by
fighting them; one or other it is impossible
to avoid, as they are not to be guided by
reason."

And again, in December, after Messrs. Tod
and Romanes had in the mean time by every
possible means endeavoured to get at the
facts, "I think you should now, without
further delay, send them answers as to the

London and Liverpool accounts, keeping
copies of them, as it will serve to amuse
Romanes in the mean time, and can do no
harm in any way."

The nephew at Carron replied to his uncle
in London, " In writing the letter to Romanes,
would it not be desirable to abstain from
entering into any minute particulars in regard
to what quantities of goods and other articles
we make, lest it should afford him a handle
for further inquiries and comparison of the
quantities of the articles with the profit made
on them ? "

Again, in January, 1827, Henry Stainton, in
London, wrote to his nephew at Carron, " We
must just let them plunge on, always giving
them calmly as little information as possible.
I think Tod and Romanes' last letter is a
very whining affair, very unlike the bold
bullying of all their former letters."

The nephew at Carron replied, " As it would
be extremely desirable for various reasons that
Romanes should not see the books, it would

perhaps be advisable yet to furnish them with a copy of that part of the statement which I sent last week, leaving the account of insurance on goods. The first thing, however, that will probably occur to Romanes will be, What can have become of such a large sum of undivided receipts? and this will lead to further questions and explanations."

. Again, in April, 1827, Henry Stainton wrote to his nephew at Carron, " I have carefully gone over the balances and adjustments you propose, of all of which I entirely approve, only I could wish the profit on the whole to be something nearer £5000, the sum at which, by conjecture, I stated it to Romanes. The shortest way would, I believe, be to add about £350 to the inventory of pig-iron; but do it in any way you think best. As the sum is so small, it cannot be of much consequence anywhere. I do not want to alarm them too much, as that might have the effect of their insisting upon having an accountant set to examine the books and details, and to report, etc., etc., for their information; and, for the same reason, I do not wish to give a *direct* refusal to any demand for papers and states that they may make, however unwilling I am to communicate any real information to them."

Later on, another outside shareholder, Mr. Jardine, applied to Joseph Dawson for information under various heads, and was treated much in the same way.

In April, 1839, Joseph Dawson, from Carron, wrote to Henry Stainton in London, " I beg to annex copy of a letter from Mr. Jardine, requiring various statements and information regarding the company, which I have little doubt you will consider it improper to furnish. I propose either to acknowledge the receipt of the letter next week, and to say that I cannot furnish the documents which he requires without the authority of a general court of the company; or I might, in the letter remitting the dividend with the abstract of the balance-sheet, say that the whole of the

accounts are included in the debits and credits
in the abstract."

Henry Stainton replied, "I think the best
way would be not to take any notice of Mr.
Jardine's letter till you send him his dividend,
with the usual abstract of the balance-sheet,
when you can, as you propose, decline furnishing the details without being authorized to do
so by a general court. Were you to write to
him sooner, he would probably stir heaven
and earth to get Sir James (Gibson Craig)
to join him in honouring us with both
his company and his questions at the meeting, which it will save you some trouble to
avoid."

Again, in October, Henry Stainton wrote to
his nephew at Carron, "I took advantage of
the comparative leisure of the country yester-
day to go over the state of the stock-ledger
balances, and proposed adjustment of some of
the accounts, comparing the whole with the
former half-years from June, 1836, and I
think you cannot do better than close the

books, as proposed, and get everything ready for the meeting. Should Mr. Jardine make his appearance, you must make the best you can of him, giving him as little information as possible."

And again, in December, "I see by the list of partners that it is as I expected, and that we will be far too heavy for Jardine, were he even able to command all the votes not in our own family, so that although he may give you some trouble he cannot ultimately be able to do any mischief."

Mr. Jardine, however, was not to be thus put off. In February, 1840, he wrote to Joesph Dawson, renewing his application for specific information, to which he maintained he was entitled, and proceeded as follows: "In the mean time, and until you show me that my opinion is erroneous, the assertion I make is, that the affairs of the company are managed by you and your near relations exactly as you think proper, without control of any sort; that the half-yearly states of the

company's affairs are not so framed as to
exhibit to the partners the real amount of
the profits, the properties belonging to the
company being stated greatly below their real
value, while the profits are made to appear
much less than the profits really made. Thus,
the amount of the debts due by the company,
as set forth in the last half-yearly balance-
sheet, is £207,163, while you admit that of
that sum £49,026 consists, not of debts due
by the company, but of sums set aside to
meet bad debts, being thus a fund belonging
to the company. Further, that under the
above aggregate sum. of debts, set forth as
due by the company, there are other two
items of £53,971 as insurance on goods, and
£59,631 as discounts and abatements.   By
transferring these large sums to the credit
and deducting them from the debit of the
company, a difference arises in favour of the
company of more than double the whole
capital. It is impossible to avoid noticing,
however disagreeable it may be to advert to

such a topic, that, while these statements
have been set forth, you and your near relations in the management have been enabled
to purchase stock during the last year at the
price of about £40,000, which, if I am at all
correct in my deductions, is far under its real
value." Mr. Jardine went on to say that, if
his statement were correct, a court of law
would order a searching investigation into the
company's affairs, with the view of obtaining
for the partners their just share of the real
profits of the company; that if he had expressed himself strongly it was from no wish
to exaggerate, but from all information being
denied to him. He added that he had thought
it right to send a copy of that letter to Sir
James Gibson Craig.

The Sir James Gibson Craig here referred
to was the company's solicitor in Edinburgh.
He was a man of great eminence, and held a
deservedly high position in his profession for
ability and integrity. On receiving a copy
of the letter, he wrote to Henry Stainton,

earnestly entreating him to give his most serious consideration to the contents.

The advice had no more effect on Henry Stainton than water on a duck's back. Mark the cool courage of the reply. He wrote to his nephew in March, " I have been thinking over the heap of rubbish Jardine has poured out in his last letter. I believe he thinks to frighten us into compliance with his wishes, as he seems to have frightened Sir J. G. Craig; but I do not feel inclined to be frightened at this great Bubbley Jock and all his noise. I would give no answer whatever to his last letter."

The nephew was not so confident, for he wrote to Henry Stainton in reply, " I have seen Sir J. G. Craig, who appears to consider Mr. Jardine's letter as a matter of the greatest importance to us, and lays great stress upon his (Jardine's) assertion, that the half-yearly abstract does not contain a fair statement of the company's affairs. He said he is quite certain that if Mr. Jardine were to bring the matter into the courts, the court would, on account of the large amount standing at the credit of discounts and abatements and insurance accounts, and to these accounts not being properly stated in the half-yearly abstracts, order the company's books to be examined for twenty or thirty years back. He also said that he considers the late sales of stock might be set aside, owing to the half-yearly abstract sent to the partners not containing the true value of the stock."

The correspondence between the managers, Sir J. G. Craig, and Mr. Jardine continued in the same strain throughout the year 1840 and for some years afterwards, Sir James urging the delivery to all the partners of full, true, and particular accounts of the affairs, funds, debts, and credits of the company, reminding the managers that the accounts rendered did not answer that description, and that whilst the other partners were kept in ignorance of the real state of the company's affairs, the managers and their relations had purchased

17

every share of stock that came into the market, and that they and the relations then held between three and four hundred shares out of the whole number taken up. But the managers coolly and calmly set all such representations at defiance.

Side by side with this correspondence affecting the outside partners, the managers were writing to each other boldly as to their internal operations amongst themselves.

After the death of Joseph Stainton in 1825, Henry Stainton, his brother, who, it will be remembered, was the manager in London, wrote in October of that year to his nephew, Joseph Dawson, the manager at Carron, "I have this morning prepared a series of minutes and resolutions to be moved at the next court. I want this business wholly off my hands, that I may get to my regular work as soon as possible." The minutes included the following proposed resolutions :—

"Resolved, that it is incumbent on this court to declare their entire approbation of the whole proceedings of the late manager in conducting the business in every respect, and further resolved to erect a monument to his memory in the churchyard of Larbert, agreeably to a design and estimate now submitted to the court, bearing the following inscription :—

" ' This monument has been erected by Carron Company to the memory of Joseph Stainton, Esq., their late manager, in testimony of their sincere gratitude for his many and important services, and of their entire approbation of the whole of his official conduct. The sum of profits divided amongst the proprietors during his management amounted to £480,000 sterling. He departed this life at Mungal Cotte, 21st February, 1825, aged 69 years. To declare this approbation in the face of all mankind.'

" Resolved, to request the present manager to keep his predecessor's line of conduct steadily in view, and to follow up all his plans and designs in such manner as shall appear to him most expedient."

There was nothing wasted in the above inscription on "In cælo quies," or "Requiescat in pace," or sentiment of that nature. Joseph Stainton's hopes and merits were based on his having divided amongst the proprietors £480,000 sterling, which, after all, was not much more than half what he ought to have divided!

Henry Stainton bettered the instruction, as has been before seen, and here are samples of some of the letters between the managers which were written on the same lines :—

In September, 1826, Joseph Dawson, at Carron, wrote to his uncle, Henry Stainton, in London, "I beg to annex a copy of the stock-ledger balances, from which you will observe that the profit for the last half-year amounts to £15,085. This we propose to reduce by transferring £2500 from flask goods to pig-iron, and reducing the value of the pig-iron inventory to that extent. Also by diminishing the inventory of flask goods £1000, and by transferring £1000 from general charges to the credit of timber, and deducting that amount from the timber inventory. This will leave £10,585 as the profit of the last six months. As this sum is still rather too much, it might be further reduced by transferring from £1000 to £1500 from general charges and flask goods to great forge and bar-iron, and by diminishing their respective inventories to the same amount, or by transferring so much to the credit of the insurance accounts."

Henry Stainton replied, "I would rather not touch the insurance accounts if you can help it, as some of the partners have their eyes upon these sums, and may think they are becoming too large to be left at rest. I prefer operating upon flask goods so extensively rather than upon general charges, as they are fully aware the profit upon the warehouses is carried to this account, and they will expect to see something from it."

Again, in January, 1827, the manager at

Carron wrote to Henry Stainton in London, " To reduce the amount of the account with the Bank of England, would it not be advisable that part of the money now in the company's hands be withdrawn and otherwise invested ? I am afraid that, if the account were produced, the balance would appear too glaring not to attract the notice of our enemies, and lead to further inquiries."

Again, in April, 1828, Henry Stainton wrote to his nephew at Carron, "It does not occur to me that there is anything objectionable in the balance as you propose to put it, unless it be that the Glasgow inventory will be rather low, as that warehouse, if I remember right, was to be valued, if necessary, at £1500."

Again, in June, the nephew wrote to the uncle, "I see no objection whatever to the entry which you propose to make to the credit of the Board of Ordnance ; but that, as a similar entry must be made in our books here, it might be difficult to give a satisfactory reason for the transfer of so large a sum, would it not be better to make it for a smaller sum at present, on account of the general dulness of the trade?"

Again, in August, Henry Stainton wrote to the nephew, "I have directed Mr. White to alter the form of his balance-sheet in the account for June, to carry away the constantly accumulating amount of profits made there. I was afraid if these accounts came to be produced at the meetings, and the large amount was seen, it might be demanded of what it consisted. Was it not unnecessary? Could it not be divided? etc., etc."

And much more in the same strain for several years afterwards.

Continuing in April, 1836, Joseph Dawson, at Carron, wrote to Henry Stainton, "I now beg to hand you a statement of the stock-ledger balances to the 31st of December last, and the way in which we propose to arrange some of the accounts."

On the 5th of the same month, Henry Stainton replied, "I am favoured with your letter of the 2nd, with the state of the balances, and of the mode in which you propose to arrange the accounts. There might have been no harm in bringing out the half-year's profit £500 more than you propose, but it may be just as you like."

Later in the same year, Henry Stainton wrote to his nephew at Carron, suggesting various alterations in the account for the then past half-year, when the profits had been very large, and proceeded, "The inventory of the blast furnaces should be put under a regular abatement of five or ten per cent. half yearly, till it is entirely reduced, and also the houses."

In other words, these valuable articles should be written down till they were made to disappear altogether.

In April, 1838, Henry Stainton wrote to his nephew at Carron, referring to some new land purchased, and said, " I approve of the entries you propose to make. It is quite right to keep an account open in the books for you new purchases. You may reduce the value when and how it may be most convenient, but they should be kept at some value so as to be kept in sight."

This purchase was accordingly "kept in sight" in the books as worth £1000. It had cost, as a matter of fact, £11,200; but there were at least ten properties not "kept in sight" at all, either in 1824 or afterwards, though worth more than £60,000 in 1824, and as many more "kept in sight" at less than their value by at least £30,000.

Sir James Gibson Craig, the company's solicitor in Edinburgh, at length, about the year 1846, began to be very much alarmed at the conduct of the managers. He had entirely disapproved of their conduct from the first. He repeated his conviction that any price which would be offered for Carron shares under the restrictions in the deed of settlement would be considerably below the value. Shares were, in fact, then for sale, and he broadly stated his opinion that it would be illegal for any managing partner to avail himself under the circumstances of the privilege of purchasing them. Becoming an old man, Sir James, in order, probably, to discharge his own conscience, in April, 1846, addressed to Joseph Dawson, the manager of the works, a letter couched in as bold language as it was possible for a solicitor to use to his client. It was as follows : " By the contract it is provided that a true, full, just, and general account of everything connected with the company shall be made up. The managing partners have exclusively the power of making up an account, and it is provided that the book in which the account is appointed to be kept shall always be open to the inspection and examination of all the partners. I have often remonstrated without effect against the total disregard, in making up the account, of the provisions of the contract. The account made up is neither true, nor full, nor just, nor general, of everything connected with the company. It does not disclose the state of the company's affairs, but conceals them. The debts due by the company are over-stated to the amount of upwards of £130,000; the assets of the company are understated by a much larger amount. Many articles, such as Bank of England and other stocks, of the value of £100,000, the value of the warehouses in London, Liverpool, Glasgow, and Leith, the shipping, etc., do not appear in the account at all. No one who is not a managing partner can have the least idea of the value of the stock, and I therefore think it illegal in any managing partner to buy the stock of any one who is not a managing partner, and who has no means of knowing the value of his stock, but is kept by the person purchasing in ignorance of it." And then Sir James went on to say that when-ever any person had the courage to apply to the court for relief the conduct of the managers would be found illegal and fraudulent.

Let the reader picture to himself the courage

of the happy family, when, on receiving this letter from their own legal adviser, the only remark upon it made by Henry Stainton, the London manager, in a letter to his nephew, was, " I am this day favoured with the copy of the extraordinary letter from Sir James Gibson Craig. I am very much inclined that Thomas (*i.e.* Thomas Dawson) should accept the shares without further ceremony, and without your taking the slightest notice of this extraordinary letter. Jardine will no doubt bark to the same tune—let him bark ! "

It should be remembered that when this strong remonstrance was written by Sir James Gibson Craig to the manager of the works, Sir James was entirely ignorant that, in addition to the concealment of property of which he was aware, the London manager had a private and concealed reserve of his own belonging to the company, and approaching a quarter of a million sterling !

As the result of the litigation which arose

out of the foregoing circumstances, the happy family in February, 1861, refunded, or rather disgorged, to the claimants, some of the ex-shareholders who had parted with their shares in ignorance of their true value, £143,750 in cash, besides returning to the representatives of deceased ex-shareholders shares and cash representing an aggregate value of about £100,000 more.

NOTES OF A VACATION TOUR.

NOTES OF A VACATION TOUR.

THE legal profession has this advantage over
other professions and occupations, that it
secures to its members a defined holiday, a
holiday regulated by statute. With the
physician, general practitioner, parson, engi-
neer, merchant, stock broker, the business of
one day of the year may be as urgent as that
of another. People are born into the world,
suffer, and die as frequently in August as in
January; the parson has his daily round, his
common task, cut out for him every day
of the calendar; the vast commercial and
monetary concerns of this kingdom must be
attended to at the moment, throughout the
year, and, like time and tide, wait for no man.
But in the profession of the law, the courts
rise early in August, not to sit again till

November, and all lawyers claim the privilege of being released from labour during that enjoyable interval; at least, it is no reproach to the most indefatigable member of that profession, and pecuniarily very little detriment to him, if he be absent during the whole of the long vacation.

Accordingly, many of us make the best use of the liberal opportunity thus placed at our disposal, and in these days of swift travelling a journey half round the world may be accomplished in the time.

Notwithstanding thirty-five years passed in the routine of professional life in London, I felt I had yet sufficient health and energy to be able to undertake a tour to Southern India, proposed to me under favourable conditions, and I successfully accomplished the object, not exactly within the limits of the long vacation, but with some moderate extension of that term.

I have not the vanity to believe that I can contribute one grain of instruction to the

public by writing about India, after five
months' rapid travelling through the country,
nor does any allusion whatever to the trip fall
strictly within the scope of " Professional
Recollections;" but it has occurred to me
that the interest of the general reader may
flag, on a perusal of cases all coming out of
a lawyer's office—they may all savour rather
too much of the " shop." Hence I ask him
to permit me to vary the subject by here
recounting a few incidents of my travels.
May I put it to him that if he will consent to
swallow the dry technicalities with which
these pages are compounded, he will, like the
good boy in the nursery, be treated with a
sweetmeat (such as it is) afterwards?

Nothing is more easy, in these days of
luxurious travelling, than a trip to India, and
the wonder is that it is not more generally
accomplished. Let the hardworked Londoner
only screw up his courage to take his berth
in one of the Peninsular and Oriental Company's steamers, sailing weekly from the

Albert Dock in London, and the rest follows almost like clockwork. Starting in October and returning in April, he will not suffer, inconveniently, from tropical heat or from annoyances caused by animal life, and he will find the Red Sea and the Indian Ocean, both going and returning, nearly as smooth as a mill-pond. He will gain his first reward for the effort at Gibraltar, where he will land for six hours or so and survey that wonder of wonders, the rock, and be introduced at one bound, as it were, from London to Spanish and Moorish life. The next halting-place will be Malta, with its double harbour and frowning fortifications. At Port Said, and afterwards at Suez, he will be brought in contact, for the first time, with Oriental life. How new to him! At Aden, he will be awestruck by the gigantic Cinder Rock, which there guards the entrance to the Red Sea as Gibraltar does the Mediterranean; and if he lands and drives four or five miles inland to the tanks or reservoirs built up between the natural ravines of the rock to store up the precious rain, which here falls only once in three years, he will meet with a teeming population of diversified nationalities, in which the noble savage holds a conspicuous place. The approach to Bombay, especially if in the morning, with the sun rising over the Ghauts, and the first view of the strikingly beautiful bay and harbour, is the climax of the voyage. All these novel and wonderful scenes may be witnessed from his home in the steamer with almost as little trouble or fatigue as from his armchair. On landing in Bombay, a new world will be opened to him, such as if he had remained content with the ordinary "Bradshaw" he never could possibly have dreamt of or realized. And from Bombay he can journey north, east, or south, by any of the lines of railway, which now, under the enlightened British rule, traverse India in all directions.

In my own case, my companion was my brother, a distinguished Oriental scholar, and as he desired to make himself better acquainted with Hindoo mythology, and also with temple architecture, the finest examples of which are found in Southern India, we crossed the continent together from Bombay to Madras, and thence journeyed, *via* Tanjore and Trichinopoly, to Madura. Afterwards, leaving the railway at Madura, we were reduced to the native mode of travelling, that is, by bullock-carts, and were jolted along over sandy tracks, not roads, at the rate of two miles an hour to the island of Paumben, at the extreme southern point of India. Let others insist on India for the Indians, or complain that we have failed to elevate or educate the natives, or have been backward in giving them Parliamentary institutions, and so forth; for myself, I humbly think that none can adequately value the inestimable benefits following in the wake of British rule in India who have not experienced, in their own proper persons, the difference between the bullock-bandy of thirty years ago and the railway of the present day.

At Paumben it might be said we had arrived at the end of the world, and we naturally asked ourselves the question how we were to get back again. Rather than retrace our steps from that remote island to Madura, and again undergo the tediousness and tortures of the bullock-cart, we chartered a native craft of the rudest build at Paumben, manned by a native crew, and provisioned with a few live fowls, some rice, and half a dozen chatty pots of water, and accomplished the transit thence to Tuticorin by sea, crossing from the latter port to Ceylon.

At Tanjore, Trichinopoly, Madura, and Tinnevelly are to be seen the finest examples of the Hindoo pagoda; but the most curious of all the temples of Southern India, inasmuch as it is more inaccessible than the others, and curiosity is excited as to how it came there, at the very southern extremity of the remote island of Paumben, is the majestic Temple of Ramiseram, resorted to by thousands of pilgrims from all parts of India. It would seem that the merit of a pilgrimage is in proportion to the distance travelled and to the hardships and difficulties of the journey, and we ourselves fell in with a weary, travel-worn pilgrim who had walked—yes, walked—the whole way from the North of India to Ramiseram, some two thousand miles or more, carrying an earthenware pot of "Ganges water" with him, in order that he might, as a pure act of devotion, pour the water over the God at Ramiseram. "Many shall come from the east and from the west," thought I to myself;—the sentence can readily be completed.

It is not my intention to inflict on the reader any description of these wonderful temples. The guide book and the Gazetteer will supply all the description he may desire. But, perhaps, I may be pardoned if, in retiring from the field of antiquity and mythology, I endeavour to reproduce two or three scenes of actual, everyday life, which interested me in the journey, and which were more in keep-

ing with my practical tastes and limited
education.

Throughout the Presidency of Madras in
1876–77, when we were there, the famine was
sore in the land. Sir William Robinson, at
whose hospitable house we were staying, told
us that a worse famine had never occurred
within his experience of upwards of thirty
years. That in Orissa, during the previous
year, was a "mere amusement" for the
officials compared to the work which had to
be done now. With this information fresh in
our ears, we drove through the town of
Madras, and along the sea-shore to witness
the celebrated surf which breaks on the shore,
not with so much force at this season as
during the monsoon. Here along the shore
and close to the pier we were brought at once
into immediate contact with startling evidence
of the famine. Thirty large steamers were
anchored in the roadstead discharging rice
brought from Calcutta. Without straining
the figure, I may say that literally there were

mountains of rice in bags already landed and heaped up on the beach. Barges and surf-boats were plying backwards and forwards between the ships and the shore, still un-lading; the railway on the pier was in active work, passing trucks on to the shore laden with bags to be added to the accumulated mountains; hundreds of native carts were arranged side by side on the shore, being promptly laden and sent off with these bags to the interior. Dense masses of the populace crowded the shore; the able-bodied actively employed in the transport, the weakly, in-cluding women and children, hanging about with baskets or small tin pots to collect the scattered grains of rice which escaped from the bags, sometimes in the interstices of the sleepers of the railway, or the planks of the pier, sometimes mixed up with the sand of the sea-shore, after the bags had been heaped up. Frequently we noticed women scrape up handfuls of sand and winnow them in a basket to separate the rice from the sand; frequently

we saw women and children take advantage
of an accidental hole in the bags, squeeze the
hole, furtively extract a few grains, hide the
half handful in their waistbands, and then
run away. There were headmen on all the
heaps of bags, and all around, armed with
canes to prevent depredation; but it went on
all the same. The beach swarmed with
people, mostly of the destitute class. We
were told that they had come from the neighbouring villages, where their natural food had
entirely failed them, to pick up what they
could in the capital. At all events, there
could be no mistake as to their condition.
Accustomed in London to appeals from professional beggars on flimsy pretexts, discarded
in a moment, I was shocked to witness the
undisguised evidence of gnawing hunger all
around us. The Government were feeding
ten thousand persons daily, and the arduous
nature of the work they had in hand may be
imagined when it is stated that the area of
famine extended to fifteen million persons.

At Tanjore we were hospitably received by Mr. Thomas, the active and efficient collector of that district. The primary duty of a collector formerly was to get in the land revenue of the territory within his jurisdiction, and hence the name. His duties now are far more comprehensive. A more appropriate name for him would be the administrator of the district, every department of which, except the judicial, is under his control. He is responsible for the peace of the district; he has to look after the roads and public buildings, the proper supply of water, the repair of tanks, bridges, and embankments, and the sanitary condition of the people; he establishes dispensaries and visits prisons; he plants and improves, and advises with the municipality, where there is one, and where there is none himself decides on the appropriation of local funds for all or any of these special objects. He sits as a magistrate, takes original charges, and hears appeals from the native magistrates and officers under him. The better to enable him to become acquainted with every part of his district, and to afford the people greater facility for representing their grievances, as well as to collect the tribute, he moves about his district in tents for eight or nine months of each year, pitching his tents in the neighbourhood of different villages, so that he may himself judge of local requirements, and that the outlying inhabitants may have personal access to him. Can any system be more paternal or better adapted to the simple childlike habits of the people of the country?

Returning from our drive one afternoon with Mr. Thomas, I observed a concourse of natives assembled in his garden. I asked who they were. He replied, "They are petitioners, all of whom have, or fancy they have, some grievance to be redressed." I said, "I suppose you have stated days for hearing these cases?" "Oh no," he replied. "Every day of the week thirty or forty persons come to me with specific complaints." I sat with him one afternoon whilst he dis-

posed of these cases. He occupied an armchair under the verandah of his house, with
his civil clerk, his magisterial clerk, and a
couple of policemen on his right, and two or
three peons, or office messengers, on his left.
A list had previously been made in writing of
all the complainants present, and a short
précis of each complaint. As each name was
called out in order, the man or woman so
summoned advanced to the foot of the collector's chair, made an obeisance, and stated
his or her grievance. There was every sort
of grievance connected with land tenure,
magisterial work, and charitable relief. It
was listened to with patience and determined
on the spot, with explanations or advice given
in the vernacular, Mr. Thomas being as conversant with Tamil as with English. It was
a domestic tribunal, intelligible and apparently
satisfactory to all concerned.

On another occasion we accompanied Mr.
Thomas on a visit of ceremony to the Ranees
of Tanjore at the palace. The Rajah of

Tanjore left no son, only a daughter, the present Princess of Tanjore, who had gone up to Delhi for the great assemblage there, when our gracious Queen was proclaimed Empress of India. He had left besides, poor man! twelve widows, who were the ranees, and who lived all together in the palace. The princess was married, but had no child. The ranees, therefore, for want of something better to do, and perhaps as much to spite the princess as for any other reason, desired to adopt a son. They could not do so without the consent of the British Government, and they petitioned for a conference with Mr. Thomas to talk the matter over. Mr. Thomas took us with him to the palace. We were received at the entrance, in Eastern fashion, by a bevy of turbaned and bedizened fellows, who constitute the idle hangers-on at all native courts, and conducted to the hall of audience, where the twelve ranees had enshrined themselves. They were not visible. A striped curtain shut off a portion of the room, in which curtain, parallel with the ground and about two feet above it, was a band of open network, about four inches wide, so that the ranees, squatted on the ground on the other side of the curtain, could peep through the network at us, but we could not see them.

We, that is, Mr. Thomas, his sub-collector, my brother, and myself, were seated round a table close to the curtain, and at the further end of the table sat the adopted son, a wretched-looking, Jewish-featured creature, dressed in white, a cap of gold tissue on his head, with nails an inch long and a complexion as yellow as his cap. Behind us, some seated, some standing, were all the tag-rag and bob-tail of the palace, looking like the chorus of warriors and nobles hired as "supers" at one shilling a night when "Othello" is performed at the Royal Italian Opera in London. The conversation was carried on briskly in Tamil between Mr. Thomas and the ranees, who seemed to hold their own all the better for being behind the curtain. It turned on the terms on which the British Government would sanction the adoption, and was conducted with equal spirit and good humour on both sides. That over, I said to Mr. Thomas in joke, "Explain to the ladies that we have come all the way from England on purpose to see them, and ask them to step out from behind the curtain and show themselves." The chief voice amongst them at once replied, "In the face of our adopted son before you, you see our faces; you must be content." An excellent answer, and we were accordingly obliged to be satisfied with the sallow, narrow-chested creature seated at the table before us.

Nothing struck me as showing our moral power in the East more than an audience of this kind. Here we were, four of us only, in the precincts of the palace of one of the oldest dynasties in Southern India, its terri-torial ambit boasting of a population of about two millions, no European troops within a

19

hundred miles of us, and yet recognized as the paramount lords of all. Wherein lies the power? The firmness and integrity of our character and the natural distrust and weakness of the native character supply the answer.

Before crossing from Tuticorin to Ceylon we ran up by the railway to Tinnevelly, where the labours of Dr. Caldwell and Dr. Serjeant, the two missionary bishops, towards the conversion of the natives to Christianity have met with marked success. A church has been built there, a spacious, airy building, capable of holding a thousand persons. Every Sunday between six and seven hundred native converts are present, the service, according to our Liturgy, being conducted in Tamil by native ordained ministers. Schools have been established in neighbouring villages, and girls educated in Mrs. Serjeant's school are sent out, after they are certificated, as superintendents of these village schools. The collector at Tinnevelly told us that there was a recent instance of a whole village having

gone over bodily to Christianity, and having
handed over their village pagoda to the mis-
sionaries. Christianity is an undoubted fact
at Tinnevelly. So is the Roman form of it
at Tuticorin, where there are two large Roman
Catholic churches, one of them nearly a
hundred years old. That church has been
apparently so contrived as to be only one
step in advance of the Hindoo pagoda. The
images at the altar are periodically painted
and dressed very much as the Hindoo god in
his holy of holies is painted and dressed;
Christian symbols are placed and enshrined
exactly after the fashion of Hindoo symbols;
processions are arranged like the Hindoo processions; between the massive buttresses
outside the church stands the car on which
the Virgin is seated and drawn, the facsimile
of the car of Vishnu, or Siva, outside the
Hindoo temple; lights, bells, flowers, rosaries,
tinfoil, perfume, are the accompaniments of
both. The Hindoo passes on to Christianity,
by these means, by very easy stages, and

finds himself transferred from one atmosphere
of symbols to another of much the same
character. The result is, that at Tuticorin,
out of a native population of twelve thousand,
one half are said to be Roman Catholics.

A bright little town is Tuticorin, seated on
the margin of the bay, and sheltered by coral
islands lying between it and the open sea.
It boasts of a pier and a good broad esplanade.
The roadstead, when we were there, was full
of ships bringing rice for famine relief and
exporting coolies to Ceylon. There is always
an average annual immigration of about three
hundred thousand coolies to Ceylon during
the coffee-picking season, but at that time
the exodus was much larger, and it answered
both purposes, relieving the famine districts
from a surplus population and furnishing
labour to the coffee cultivators in Ceylon,
who were then unusually prosperous. The
coasting schooners were carrying the coolies
across, packed as thick as herrings, at two
rupees a head, regardless of cholera, which

was virulent in the town. There was plenty of life, as may be imagined, on the shore, boats crammed full of coolies going off to the schooners for immigration, and the fleet of trading vessels at anchor discharging into boats their full cargoes of bags of rice for the famine districts, the boats plying backwards and forwards between the ships and the shore in active work suited. to the pressing emergency of the occasion.

Few there are, even in short journeys from home, who have not occasionally come across novel and interesting characters. On our way from Tinnevelly back to Tuticorin, we changed carriages at the junction, and on the main line got into a saloon carriage, whose only occupant was a stout, good-looking Englishman of about fifty years of age. He had light, chestnut, curly hair, carefully parted in the middle, and a handsome beard and moustache. He was in his shirt-sleeves, reclining on one of the long seats of the carriage, and on the opposite seat was laid out a complete series of dishes, containing cold fowl, salad, bread, pudding, plantains, with all suitable accompaniments of butter, salt, pepper, etc.

Directly we appeared at the door he pulled himself together, and apologized for monopolizing the carriage, " Come in, pray come in; I've just finished my tiffin. I'll put all these things by into my tiffin-basket in a moment. Try one of these plantains; the red ones are riper than the yellow—you'll find them excellent." So saying, he collected his dishes, emptied the bones and *débris* out of the carriage window, and packed the utensils in a large wicker tiffin-basket, covered with leather, which was evidently his carefully-contrived and constant travelling companion. Having done that, he put on his clean white jacket with gilt uniform buttons, combed his handsome beard with a tortoiseshell pocket comb, kept in his pocket for the purpose, and began to talk freely.

He had come from Lahore, he said ; thence

to Calcutta, and on rather rapidly to Madras, stopping here and there. He slept last night at Madura, and was going for the night to the Traveller's Bungalow, at Tuticorin, intending to cross the next day in the British India Steam Navigation Company's steamship *Arabia* to Ceylon. " No," I observed, " you cannot go to the Traveller's Bungalow at Tuticorin to-night; it has already been engaged by my brother and myself." " That's unlucky," he replied; " then I suppose I must sleep in the verandah." He was, however, so good-humoured about it, that I rejoined, " No, you must not do that ; you shall have my room, and I will have a bed put up in my brother's room." And that was eventually done.

" Now who can you be ? " I asked of myself; " but for a slight excess of freedom in manner and talkativeness, I should take you for a general officer on a tour of inspection." This idea was negatived by his telling us that he lived in London, and had been out to India every year for the last five years, landing at Bombay and making the round of all the Presidencies. "Ah! I see," again guessed I to myself, "you must be a traveller for some mercantile house in England; perhaps an agent for the sale of brandy or beer, or light wines or provisions." The elaborate tiffin-basket rather encouraged that conjecture.

On arriving at Tuticorin we parted, and I went off to Underwood, the agent for the steamer, to secure our passage to Colombo. Whilst I was so engaged, in walked our stout handsome friend for the same purpose. "Oh, Mr. Underwood," he exclaimed, on entering the office, "is that you? Don't you remember me, Captain McQueen, formerly a skipper in the Peninsular and Oriental service? Don't you remember coming home with me in the *Moultan* from China?" Here, then, was one important point solved. Our friend was Captain McQueen, formerly a commander in the Peninsular and Oriental Steam Navigation Company's service. We returned together to

the wretched Traveller's Bungalow in Tuticorin, and I made him comfortable in my
room there. From thence we adjourned to
the little club in the town, where, notwithstanding his substantial repast in the railway
carriage, he joined us for tiffin, going through
a second meal under that name, as if he had
tasted nothing all day. We all dined together
at the club in the evening, and he had the
talk nearly all to himself. Ships, trade,
politics, people of all ranks whom he had
sailed with, every conceivable subject, inter-
spersed with remarks on the food, quick calls
for this or that dish, and a joke now and then
with his man-servant Pedro in bad Hindustani.

The next morning early we walked down
together to the beach, and embarked in the
native bullion boat which took us off to the
Arabia, anchored, owing to the shoal water,
six or seven miles from shore. He was one of
the only three or four passengers on board the
vessel. Nevertheless, he was brisk enough to
take the best cabin, had the first bath, and

secured the best of everything for himself, without any show of selfishness but yet like a practical traveller. In conversation with him on board the *Arabia*, I frequently led up to the difficulty which still puzzled me, and which I propounded silently to myself as I looked at him, "You were formerly in the Peninsular and Oriental service; what are you now?" By way of a mild leading question, I said to him, "You were not sorry, I suppose, to leave the service?" "Delighted," he replied; "I had had enough of it. The company cut down our pay. In my time a captain had £1200 a year pay, and the best of living on board free. What do you think now? Why, actually, every officer has to pay for his own liquor; he can't have a bottle of beer without he pays for it. I couldn't stand that. Now I'm my own master, and have my own independent occupation." Then he branched off into some other topic, talking all the time with great shrewdness and good humour.

We anchored off Colombo early the follow-

ing morning. I was on deck long before sun-
rise. The whole range of mountains running
inland forty or fifty miles from the coast, including Adam's Peak, was distinctly visible
before the sun showed itself above the horizon.
As we approached, the spicy breezes from the
island were wafted to the ship, inviting us to
land. On coming to anchor, I asked Captain
McQueen if he was going on shore. "No,"
he replied, "not yet. I shall have my break-
fast comfortably on board; the purser here on
this ship gives capital breakfasts; then I shall
land, and take the afternoon train to Kandy.
I've got some business at Kandy." So we left
him, and remained ourselves some days in
Colombo, going on afterwards to Kandy.

The rail from Colombo to Kandy runs along
the flat for nearly three hours, and then com-
mences the ascent of the mountain. With a
bogie engine in front and another behind, the
train winds, in rapid serpentine curves, up the
incline, occasionally overhanging a perpen-
dicular cliff, and overlooking at every turn a

vast expanse of country, clothed with tropical vegetation, until it attains an altitude of about 1800 feet, and then it runs level to Kandy. The incline is about twelve miles in length, and the gradient throughout one in forty-five. The ascent, following closely alongside of the old admirably engineered wheel-road, with its foreground of rocks and trees draped with luxuriant parasites and creepers, its varied and distant views, is quite one of the most remarkable sights of the island. Kandy itself is beautifully situated in the centre of an amphitheatre of mountains, and being the seat of the Government for a portion of the year, all the surroundings are well cared for. A large sheet of ornamental water sparkles in close proximity to the town, and stretches away far beyond its limits. The open spaces, roads, and walks, in and around the town are laid out with an eye to the picturesque, and are carefully maintained. The temple containing the sacred tooth of Buddha stands near the margin of the water, and terminates the vista

formed by the small green pleasure-ground
which leads up to it. We could not see the
tooth itself—that is a privilege reserved for a
very few. Disappointed curiosity may ask
with as much reason as spleen, what is there
to see in it? But we saw the bell-shaped
gold cover, overlaid with precious stones, one
of nine similar covers one within the other,
which contains the tooth, the nine covers to
be opened only on very special occasions, and
then by three separate keys, each key being
in the possession of a separate custodian. *Le
jeu ne vaut pas la chandelle.*

The Botanical Gardens of Peradinia are
within an easy walk of the town, and there in
those gardens may be seen in vigorous growth
splendid groups of the giant bamboo, the
mahogany tree, upas tree, the Talipot palm,
with its ragged stem, various kinds of gam-
boge, the cinnamon tree, the magnificent
Indian-rubber tree, some of these trees being
a hundred feet high and twenty feet in girth—
so different from our slender drawing-room

plant,—the cocoa tree, cardamom, clove; in
short, acres on acres of our choicest hot-house
vegetation, all growing in the open air. The
Talipot palm, I was told, arrives at maturity
in about forty years, flowers for the first and
only time when at maturity, and then dies.
This fair world can boast of many bright and
lovely spots; but let the traveller, especially if
fresh from London, stroll out at night, as I
did, by the margin of the lake at Kandy and
round the green, gaze on the brilliant starlit
sky, Orion's belt immediately over head, Sirius
and Canopus shining like moons, with a galaxy
of bright stars studded thickly in the heavens;
below the fire-flies flitting about in myriads in
the soft warm balmy air, the lights of the
bungalows on the hills reflected in the water,
and he will irresistibly exclaim, "This is
indeed a scene of surpassing beauty!"

Well, on arriving at Kandy, the first person
we met on entering the hotel was our friend,
Captain McQueen, dressed as usual in a complete suit of pure white, with his diamond

ring on his third finger, his radiant face and
curly hair and beard looking more captivating
than ever. " Oh ! " he exclaimed, " I am so
glad to see you ; you'll find this hotel a very
good one ; the butler is a friend of mine, he
will look after you." We had some further
conversation. He was going off, he said, to
some friends twenty miles off, but would return
to Kandy ; thence he was going to Galle, and
would in time take the steamer to Madras,
and work his way eventually round to Bombay.
I was impressed with the energy and " go "
involved in the whole programme, and to think
that the same circuit of the whole of India
had been made by him annually for the last
five years ! But in what cause ? " Perhaps as
a commercial traveller or commission agent,"
still thought I to myself. " If so, with your
energy, good appearance, and good address, I
doubt not you will sell thousands of pounds'
worth of brandy or tinned soups, or whatever
else you travel in, and make a good thing of
it." He went off in a carriage and pair for his

twenty mile journey, and, meanwhile, we made an excursion to the mountain sanitarium of Newera Ellia, and there enjoyed a few nights of sharp cold, with morning hoar frosts, at an altitude of about 6500 feet above the level of the sea.

On our return to Kandy we took up our old quarters at the hotel, and sat down to the *table d'hôte* dinner in the evening. Captain McQueen had returned also, and occupied the only vacant chair next to me, talking as usual about everything and everybody, with observations thrown in parenthetically about the dinner: "Why, what's this?—tinned salmon? Here's a bottle of anchovy, but where's the melted butter? Here, Pedro, send the butler to me. My good man" (to the butler), "always serve melted butter with fish—not now, I can do without it; give me some of that cold butter, but in future, remember, always melted butter; anchovy cannot be taken alone." Then the conversation diverged about his movements, and why he could not come with us to Newera Ellia because he had business at this place and that.

At last my curiosity got the better of my good manners, and I said to him right out, "Pray, may I ask, Captain McQueen, what business you are now engaged in?"

"Oh!" he replied, smiling, "I'm an ordained minister."

"An ordained minister!" I echoed, unable to conceal my astonishment.

"Yes," he rejoined, "I really am, but I don't look like one;" and seeing that my surprise had not subsided, "I hope you don't think that cheerfulness and sociability are inconsistent with such a calling."

"By no means," I replied heartily. "I believe that these qualities and Christianity are convertible terms. But may I ask, are you an ordained minister of the Church of England?"

"Oh no," he replied; "I am an ordained minister of the Catholic Apostolic Church in Gordon Square. My mission to India every year is to visit and pray with the scattered members of that communion. But though we believe in one communion, we are not bigots; we recognize no denominations, and object to any designation which implies sectarianism; all Christians are alike to us. My immediate business, however, is with persons in India in direct connection with the Catholic Apostolic Church, and I am sent from Gordon Square to keep alive in its scattered members the true Catholic spirit of Christianity. I have some members here in Kandy, two or three private soldiers of the 57th Regiment. I have been praying with them this morning. I have a few members at every place I visit, and I seek them out and pray with them individually."

He then shortly and earnestly expounded to me his creed, and by his frequent reference to the second Advent, the Four beasts, the Spirit and the Bride, I gathered that he drew his inspiration chiefly from the Book of Revelation.

Except for the fact that he had not before given us the slightest clue to his vocation, there was in truth no ground for surprise. Why should not the Church in Gordon Square have its travelling priest or missionary? Rather should we do honour to a fervent body of Christians, numerically small, who can devote so considerable a portion of their temporal goods to maintain the spirit of religion amongst their countrymen in distant lands, and to the individual who can leave his home and sacrifice his well-earned ease with that object, who, though imbued with the spirit of Xavier, may not think it necessary for the success of his cause to wear the hair shirt of the saint.

Returning from Ceylon to Bombay, we enjoyed what might be called a yachting voyage of a delightful kind, in one of the coasting steamers of the British India Steam Navigation Company. This vessel, picking us up at Colombo, ran northward along the Malabar coast, anchoring, to discharge and take in cargo, at Colachel, Allipey, Cochin, Beypore, Calicut, Budagherry, Tillicherry, Cannanore, Mangalore, Carwar, Goa, and Rutnagherry. Can any list of places sound more attractive than these, or, in fact, equal them in interest, when the ease with which they can thus be visited be considered ? At each place the vessel remained sufficient time to admit of our landing and roaming about for five or six hours. Each place possesses a character of its own, the inhabitants, costumes, boats, and merchandise of each differing more or less from the others, so that the interest of the voyage is kept up throughout. The magnificent outline of the Western Ghauts, which stretch north and south the whole way from Cape Comorin to Bombay, is in view from first to last, the changing shadows on the mountains affording a constant treat to the eye ; whilst, as far as Cochin, may be seen, sparkling in the sunlight, villages, churches, and chapels, dotted all along the coast, the Syrian Christians having settlements there, besides the Roman Catholics.

Allipey and Tillicherry, out-of-the-way places, I had visited before, and there the record of my former visit begins and ends, for I was only six years of age when my father and mother brought me home with them from India in the ship *Ogle Castle*, five hundred tons burden, long prior to the days of steam and of the Red Sea route. The ship on that occasion touched at both those places to take in a cargo of pepper, and I can vaguely remember the native boats coming alongside, and the bags of coarse matting which contained the pepper being hoisted on board, and its pungent smell. We were upwards of five months performing the voyage home, and were nearly lost, pepper and all, in a gale of wind off the Azores. Strange the feeling of recognition, the dream-like feeling, which came over me on my second visit to Tillicherry and Allipey at finding the same scene, the same boats, the same cargo, the same odour, again brought before me after the lapse of so many years !

Cochin, the capital of the feudatory state of the same name, is situated on the shore of a backwater, or lagoon, about a hundred miles in length, formed by the torrents flowing from the Western Ghauts, and approached from the sea by a narrow and shallow entrance, and bounded on all sides by cocoa-nut trees. When once the canoe, with passengers from the steamer, shoots through this entrance, the wide lagoon opens out, and the town of Cochin comes immediately into view. A very interesting place it is, for many reasons—from its position on this large expanse of inland water, enlivened by the traffic of native trading craft of the most primitive shape and construction; from the numerous Roman Catholic chapels visible at various points of the shore; from the rude old Portuguese building, with its massive buttresses, containing the tomb of Vasco da Gama, and now used for their church by the Protestant portion of the community; and lastly, from the colony of black and white Jews who settled here two or three centuries ago,

who still preserve their characteristic physiognomy, keep to their own quarter, and have
their rabbis, synagogues, schools, customs,
and services, as separate and apart as if living
in a world of their own.

We had time to hire a boat from the Cochin
jetty and pull up the backwater for about two
miles to the Jews' colony. We were fortunate
enough (it being their Sabbath) to find service
just commencing in one of the synagogues.
Numerous unmistakable Jews had assembled,
clothed in long flowing garments of silk of
the most brilliant colours—crimson, purple,
emerald green, striped, etc. In the centre of
the square room which formed the synagogue,
and which was hung with chandeliers and oil
lamps, there was a roomy open pulpit, into
which, after a time, one rabbi, and then three
together, entered, veiled themselves and stood.
Then was brought out to them, with ceremony,
from a closet over what we should call the
altar, a cylindrical case containing a double
roll of parchment, the Book of the Law, from

which the rabbis read, intoning, the congregation, also veiled, responding. This was followed by silent prayer, the congregation standing in rows, and all facing towards the altar. Then the parchment roll was restored to the case, the congregation gathering round it to kiss or touch it before it was put back into the closet. I leave it to others more conversant with the subject to say whether the forms observed by this remote and isolated little community correspond with the ritual of those of the same faith at home.

The Portuguese town of Goa, the glory of which has departed, but which once ranked high in importance among the cities of Western India, would have well repaid the trouble of a visit, and I was disappointed to find that it was six miles up the Goa river, too far off to enable us to make the excursion there and back during the short time the steamer was anchored at the mouth of the river.

Soon after landing in Bombay we left it

again for Ellora, in the dominions of the
Nizam. It is an out-of-the-way place, reached
by a night's journey by rail from Bombay to
Nandgaum, and thence on wheels of some sort
for about fifty miles of road to Roza, the
Mahommedan town, situated on the tableland
of the high range of hills in the face of which
are the celebrated caves. Sir Salar Jung had
given orders that my brother should be assisted
in his visit to the caves, and that a tonga,
which is a kind of pony curricle much used in
India, especially in the hills, with relays of
ponies, should be ready to convey us from the
station at Nandgaum to Roza. Unluckily,
the tongas had been previously engaged by
some officers of the contingent at Arungabad,
and we were doomed to perform the road
journey from Nandgaum to Roza in my old
enemy the bullock-bandy. For fifteen hours
we were incarcerated in these wretched
vehicles, that is, from three a.m., when we
left the station at Nandgaum, until six p.m.
the same evening, when we arrived at Roza.

As soon as it was daylight I could see that we were jogging along over a most uninteresting, flat, arid, famine-stricken country, with nothing worthy of notice except the miserable, flat-roofed, mud villages, at which we changed bullocks, and occasionally a herd of black buck in the distance. It was all the Nizam's territory after the first ten miles from Nandgaum, and we had for the whole distance an escort of a couple of his highness's mounted sowars, intended, oh, mockery! as a guard of honour, who walked their horses at a foot's pace the whole way by the side of the bullocks. I swore by all the Hindoo gods (not a binding oath seeing that I do not believe in them) that no sight on the face of the earth, or inside it, would ever induce me to enter a bullock-bandy again; but when I saw Ellora, and the wonderful monuments of human industry and art which were there exhibited to my view, I soon forgot my former anguish.

At Roza we were met by Mr. Burgess, the antiquary, who was engaged in collecting

materials for writing an account of the Ellora
Caves, and by the agents of Sir Salar Jung,
who had prepared a bungalow for our recep-
tion. The town of Roza is essentially
Mahommedan, and has been built of solid
rectangular stones brought from the ancient
city of Tagara, but is itself now falling into
ruins. Within the cupolaed walls is the tomb
of Aurungzebe, plain and open to the sky,
but entered through doors of perforated
marble. The other tombs, within and without the walls, are of different holy men and
kings of Hyderabad, all constructed with a
central dome, flanked by minarets, and very
beautiful in form and execution. Many of
the stone slabs at the entrance to these tombs
were inlaid with lumps of agate, glass, and
coloured stones, as votive offerings from
various individuals, and against the doors
were nailed horseshoes, with a like object.
We, in England, have the same custom with
regard to horseshoes, and Mr. Burgess was of
opinion that it was introduced into England

by the Crusaders. In the East, it is an offering by a soldier who has been promoted to a rank which entitles him to keep a horse.

Descending from the plateau of Roza to the face of the hill, we came upon the caves of Ellora. They are cut in the face of the amphitheatre of trap-hills which rises abruptly out of the plain, and extends in a semicircle for about two miles. They are sixty-five in number, the earliest in date, about A.D. 300, being Buddhist, cut in the southern horn of the semicircular range; the next or intermediate, both in place and date, being Brahminical or Hindoo; and the most modern, about A.D. 900, being Jain, cut in the northern horn of the range. The trap formation of the hill, consisting of large horizontal slabs of rock, is favourable to excavation, the slabs forming naturally the floor and roof of the temple. Many of the temples run for nearly two hundred feet into the solid rock, and are two or three floors in height, supported by pillars of the most exquisite design and execution, and all round the walls are bass-reliefs, illustrating the gods of the Hindoo mythology, in almost every phase of their history.

There is one temple at Ellora which, unlike the others, is not a cave or a cavern, but a vast independent structure, standing out in the open, as if built stone upon stone, according to the most approved principles of architecture. Yet, can it be believed, that this wonderful temple, a hundred feet in height, and covering an area nearly equal to that of our Royal Exchange in London, is not built at all. Not built! How, then, can it have attained the proportions thus presented to the eye? Actually the temple itself, with its obelisks, colossal elephants, and subsidiary temples standing all around it, is hewn entirely out of the solid rock, from which it is wholly separate and apart, as much as St. Paul's is from the houses which surround it. And within the temple, its hall, vestibules, galleries, storeys and staircases have been scooped out, so to speak, and together with the detail of carving, which covers every part of the outside and inside, are as much part of the marvel as the edifice itself. The race of Hindoos who designed, and with such indomitable perseverance executed, this wonderful work must have been very different from the apathetic and indolent Hindoos of the present day. This temple is called Kailasa, and the date of it about A.D. 700.

Accompanied by Sir Salar Jung's agents, we left Roza, this time not in a bullock-bandy, but in a tonga, and after a pleasant drive, owing to the brisk air, arrived at the fortress of Dowlutabad, at which we halted on our way to Aurungabad. Of all impregnable places, at all events before the invention of the 100-ton gun, Dowlutabad must surely rank the first. Picture to yourself a tall wedding cake, placed on a flat dining-room table, and an army of pigmies an inch high marching to capture the sugar ornament at the top of the cake. That ornament is the fortress at the top of the rock, which rises perpendicularly out of the plain—an inland Gibraltar, in fact. It is absolutely inaccessible except through an extensive circumvallation outside, and inside through zigzag passages cut out of the solid rock, capable of admitting only two or three abreast, commanded by positions which would be fatal to the assaulting column, with precautions by means of iron doors and furnaces for shutting in and roasting the head of the column should it have advanced beyond a certain point. It is not easy to imagine such a combination of natural and artificial defences.

From this remarkable place we proceeded to Aurungabad, the chief object of interest in which is the Taj, or marble tomb of Aurungzebe's wife, said to be an imitation of the Taj at Agra. The town itself, however, is worth visiting, being very native in character. Whilst sitting in the verandah of the bungalow with the Nizam's collector, or district officer, an educated native, speaking English fluently, I asked him whether he would prefer serving under the British Government or under the Nizam. "Under the Nizam," he replied. "Why?" "I will tell you," he said. "Your countrymen are apt to assume a superiority of race when they are put over us, to be exclusive and often overbearing and arrogant in their manner towards us; on that account I would rather work with my own people, even for less pay."

Thus conversing, the public tonga, going to Nandgaum, drove up with a young officer belonging to the contingent seated in it as sole passenger, the rest of the vehicle being piled up with his luggage. We had arranged to send our native servant by the same conveyance, and as it drew up the man attempted to get in. The officer resented the apparent intrusion, and peremptorily said there was no room, and that the man must follow the next day. "See," observed my friend the collector, turning towards me, "there is an example of what I was just saying to you. Your native servant has an equal right to a

seat in that tonga, but he is ordered off as if
he was so much dirt." I confessed that the
case was in point for his purpose; nevertheless, we came to the rescue, insisted on our
man going in the tonga, and carried the day.
The same afternoon, after our drive through
the town, we assembled again in the same
bungalow, and sat down to dinner, inviting
the collector to join us at table. "No," he
replied; "I cannot eat with you. We are
forbidden to do that; I should lose caste.
Pray excuse me." I was glad of the opportunity of teaching him a little lesson out of
his own book, and pointed out to him, in
perfect good humour, that he was now himself assuming a superiority over us, and that
the exclusiveness was not all on our side.

Returning to Bombay, little remained but
to prepare for our voyage home. These preparations, of course, included a few purchases
as mementoes for friends at home. "Where-
soever the body is, thither will the eagles
be gathered together" is applicable to the

Englishman just previous to his departure from India to return to his native country. The borahs, or native pedlars, scent their prey from afar with the keen instinct of the eagle or kite. They seldom go near the old-established denizen, knowing that he, as a permanent fixture, has become callous to the articles of art or ornament which come within the category of presents, and is too busy to encumber himself with such things. But the traveller homeward bound has to think of his sisters, his cousins, and his aunts, all of whom on his return will be expecting a special memento of some kind from a land, the textile fabrics, embroideries, jewellery, and ornaments of which are so much appreciated at home. The news has spread that there is a sahib stopping at such a bungalow on Malabar Hill, intending to return to England by the next steamer. Immediately the borahs are gathered together, intent, not on spoliating him—perhaps that is too strong a word—but on tempting him with every sort of Eastern commodity which they think, and think rightly, will be acceptable to the ladies at home.

Quite an Indian institution is the borah, in a country where shops are scarce. He is himself the peripatetic shop. Dressed in pure flowing white, with a compact white turban on his head, his forehead neatly marked in red or yellow ochre with the distinctive mark of his creed, and a handsome turquoise ring on his finger, he enters the compound of the bungalow, followed by two or three coolies, each carrying an enormous pack on his head. He speaks English, and politely salaaming, approaches the open verandah, where the family may be seated, with "Master want any Cashmere goods, Rampoor Chudder shawls, silks? I got all new goods; master, look, master need not buy." The coolies advance, deposit their loads, retire, and seat themselves on their haunches at the further extremity of the verandah. Then pack No. 1 is untied by the clever borah, the contents

21—2

taken out one by one, and strewn by degrees on the floor of the verandah in rich profusion. Meanwhile he has squatted himself on the floor, and by his calm dignified manner and skilful comments on his goods as he exhibits them piecemeal has impressed the bystanders with a belief—not always well-founded—that he is honest and trustworthy. If a bargain be attempted, a price offered less than the price asked, he replies, with an air of offended dignity, "I make one price, five per cent. on my goods, not more. Master not like me to have two prices." Then, in admired confusion, pack No. 2 is untied, and gorgeous table and chair-covers are brought out and unfolded, some worked in gold and silver from Delhi, some from Hyderabad in Scinde, slippers embroidered in like manner, dressing-gowns of soft Cashmere wool, beetle-wing ornaments, all of which are piled up on the shawls, Dacca muslins and brocades of the former pack, until the verandah is literally heaped up with beautiful things. Who can resist such temptation, or the calm face and dignified assurance of the accomplished borah? I can think of no pleasure so perfect and enjoyed with such absolute ease and tranquility as reclining in a cane armchair in a spacious verandah, under a temperature of about 80°, looking languidly at the beautiful Eastern things which the borah brings out one by one out of his pack and holds up for approval, the dialogue being conducted by a council of ladies, who, seated around in other armchairs, pass their comments on such articles as are peculiarly within their province, provided always that your bankers' book shows a good balance to your credit. The purchases over, but not till several hours have thus been whiled away, the borah folds up his goods, replaces them in the packs, which are tied up, and he and the coolies walk away from the precincts as they came.

Bidding adieu to many kind friends in Bombay, we re-embarked for England, and the beautiful flashing light of " The Prongs," off Colaba Point, gradually fading away in the distance, was my last sight of India, as the *Surat* ploughed her way through the darkness of the ocean on our homeward voyage.

THE END.

PRINTED BY WILLIAM CLOWES AND SONS, LIMITED,
LONDON AND BECCLES.   *S. & H.*

CPSIA information can be obtained at www.ICGtesting.com
Printed in the USA
BVOW02s1452110416

443790BV00006B/31/P